I, Luke

I, Luke

*Being a Summary of Eyewitness Reports
Concerning Jesus Christ*

By Luke the Physician

TRANSLATED BY KENNETH TAYLOR

OUR SUNDAY VISITOR, INC. / *Huntington*

Copyright © 1981 by Our Sunday Visitor, Inc.
ALL RIGHTS RESERVED
Library of Congress Catalog Card No. 81-80713
ISBN 0-87973-665-8
Verses are taken from the *Living Bible,* copyright © 1971 by Tyndale House
Publishers, Wheaton, Illinois. Used by permission.
Nihil obstat: Rev. Lawrence Gollner
Imprimatur: ✠ *Leo A. Pursley, Bishop of Fort Wayne-South Bend*
January 9, 1976
Design by Paul Zomberg
Illustrations by James McIlrath
PRINTED IN THE UNITED STATES OF AMERICA

1   2   3   4   5   6   7   8   9   10   90   89   87   86   85   84   83   82   81

Most Excellent Theophilus,

DEAR FRIEND WHO LOVES GOD: Several biographies of Christ have already been written using as their source material the reports circulating among us from the early disciples and other eyewitnesses. However, it occurred to me that it would be well to recheck all these accounts from first to last and after thorough investigation to pass this summary on to you, to reassure you of the truth of all you were taught.

LUKE

CHAPTER ONE

The Proper Time

MY STORY begins with a Jewish priest, Zacharias, who lived when Herod was king of Judea. Zacharias was a member of the Abijah division of the Temple service corps. (His wife Elizabeth was, like himself, a member of the priest tribe of the Jews, a descendant of Aaron.) Zacharias and Elizabeth were godly folk, careful to obey all of God's laws in spirit as well as in letter. But they had no children, for Elizabeth was barren; and now they were both very old.

One day as Zacharias was going about his work in the Temple—for his division was on duty that week—the honor fell to him by lot to enter the inner sanctuary and burn incense before the Lord. Meanwhile, a great crowd stood outside in the Temple court, praying as they always did during that part of the service when the incense was being burned.

Zacharias was in the sanctuary when suddenly an angel appeared, standing to the right of the altar of incense! Zacharias was startled and terrified.

But the angel said, "Don't be afraid, Zacharias! For I have come to tell you that God has heard your prayer, and your wife

Elizabeth will bear you a son! And you are to name him John. You will both have great joy and gladness at his birth, and many will rejoice with you. For he will be one of the Lord's great men. He must never touch wine or hard liquor—and he will be filled with the Holy Spirit, even from before his birth! And he will persuade many a Jew to turn to the Lord his God. He will be a man of rugged spirit and power like Elijah, the prophet of old; and he will precede the coming of the Messiah, preparing the people for his arrival. He will soften adult hearts to become like little children's, and will change disobedient minds to the wisdom of faith."

Zacharias said to the angel, "But this is impossible! I'm an old man now, and my wife is also well along in years."

Then the angel said, "I am Gabriel! I stand in the very presence of God. It was he who sent me to you with this good news! And now, because you haven't believed me, you are to be stricken silent, unable to speak until the child is born. For my words will certainly come true at the proper time."

Meanwhile the crowds outside were waiting for Zacharias to appear and wondered why he was taking so long. When he finally came out, he couldn't speak to them, and they realized from his gestures that he must have seen a vision in the Temple. He stayed on at the Temple for the remaining days of his Temple duties and then returned home. Soon afterward Elizabeth his wife became pregnant and went into seclusion for five months.

"How kind the Lord is," she exclaimed, "to take away my disgrace of having no children!"

The following month God sent the angel Gabriel to Nazareth, a village in Galilee, to a virgin, Mary, engaged to be married to a man named Joseph, a descendant of King David.

Gabriel appeared to her and said, "Congratulations, favored lady! The Lord is with you!"

Confused and disturbed, Mary tried to think what the angel could mean.

2

"Don't be frightened, Mary," the angel told her, "for God has decided to bless you wonderfully! Very soon now, you will become pregnant and have a baby boy, and you are to name him 'Jesus.' He shall be very great and shall be called the Son of God. And the Lord God shall give him the throne of his ancestor David. And he shall reign over Israel forever; his Kingdom shall never end!"

Mary asked the angel, "But how can I have a baby? I am a virgin."

The angel replied, "The Holy Spirit shall come upon you, and the power of God shall overshadow you; so the baby born to you will be utterly holy—the Son of God. Furthermore, six months ago your Aunt Elizabeth—'the barren one,' they called her—became pregnant in her old age! For every promise from God shall surely come true."

Mary said, "I am the Lord's servant, and I am willing to do whatever he wants. May everything you said come true." And then the angel disappeared.

A few days later Mary hurried to the highlands of Judea to the town where Zacharias lived, to visit Elizabeth.

At the sound of Mary's greeting, Elizabeth's child leaped within her and she was filled with the Holy Spirit.

She gave a glad cry and exclaimed to Mary, "You are favored by God above all other women, and your child is destined for God's mightiest praise. What an honor this is, that the mother of my Lord should visit me! When you came in and greeted me, the instant I heard your voice, my baby moved in me for joy! You believed that God would do what he said; that is why he has given you this wonderful blessing."

Mary responded, "Oh, how I praise the Lord. How I rejoice in God my Savior! For he took notice of his lowly servant girl, and now generation after generation forever shall call me blest of God. For he, the mighty Holy One, has done great things to me. His mercy goes on from generation to generation, to all who reverence him.

"How powerful is his mighty arm! How he scatters the proud and haughty ones! He has torn princes from their thrones and exalted the lowly. He has satisfied the hungry hearts and sent the rich away with empty hands. And how he has helped his servant Israel! He has not forgotten his promise to be merciful. For he promised our fathers—Abraham and his children—to be merciful to them forever."

Mary stayed with Elizabeth about three months and then went back to her own home.

By now Elizabeth's waiting was over, for the time had come for the baby to be born—and it was a boy. The word spread quickly to her neighbors and relatives of how kind the Lord had been to her, and everyone rejoiced.

When the baby was eight days old, all the relatives and friends came for the circumcision ceremony. They all assumed the baby's name would be Zacharias, after his father.

But Elizabeth said, "No! He must be named John!"

"What?" they exclaimed. "There is no one in all your family by that name." So they asked the baby's father, talking to him by gestures.

He motioned for a piece of paper and to everyone's surprise wrote, "His name is *John!*" Instantly Zacharias could speak again, and he began praising God.

Wonder fell upon the whole neighborhood, and the news of what had happened spread through the Judean hills. And everyone who heard about it thought long thoughts and asked, "I wonder what this child will turn out to be? For the hand of the Lord is surely upon him in some special way."

Then his father Zacharias was filled with the Holy Spirit and gave this prophecy:

"Praise the Lord, the God of Israel, for he has come to visit his people and has redeemed them. He is sending us a Mighty Savior from the royal line of his servant David, just as he promised through his holy prophets long ago—someone to save us from our enemies, from all who hate us.

"He has been merciful to our ancestors, yes, to Abraham himself, by remembering his sacred promise to him, and by granting us the privilege of serving God fearlessly, freed from our enemies, and by making us holy and acceptable, ready to stand in his presence forever.

"And you, my little son, shall be called the prophet of the glorious God, for you will prepare the way for the Messiah. You will tell his people how to find salvation through forgiveness of their sins. All this will be because the mercy of our God is very tender, and heaven's dawn is about to break upon us, to give light to those who sit in darkness and death's shadow, and to guide us to the path of peace."

The little boy greatly loved God and when he grew up he lived out in the lonely wilderness until he began his public ministry to Israel.

CHAPTER TWO

The Most Joyful News

ABOUT THIS TIME Caesar Augustus, the Roman Emperor, decreed that a census should be taken throughout the nation. (This census was taken when Quirinius was governor of Syria.)

Everyone was required to return to his ancestral home for this registration. And because Joseph was a member of the royal line, he had to go to Bethlehem in Judea, King David's ancient home—journeying there from the Galilean village of Nazareth. He took with him Mary, his fiancée, who was obviously pregnant by this time.

And while they were there, the time came for her baby to be born; and she gave birth to her first child, a son. She wrapped him in a blanket and laid him in a manger, because there was no room for them in the village inn.

That night some shepherds were in the fields outside the village, guarding their flocks of sheep. Suddenly an angel appeared among them, and the landscape shone bright with the glory of the Lord. They were badly frightened, but the angel reassured them.

"Don't be afraid!" he said. "I bring you the most joyful news ever announced, and it is for everyone! The Savior—yes, the Messiah, the Lord—has been born tonight in Bethlehem! How will you recognize him? You will find a baby wrapped in a blanket, lying in a manger!"

Suddenly, the angel was joined by a vast host of others—the armies of heaven—praising God:

"Glory to God in the highest heaven," they sang, "and peace on earth for all those pleasing him."

When this great army of angels had returned again to heaven, the shepherds said to each other, "Come on! Let's go to Bethlehem! Let's see this wonderful thing that has happened, which the Lord has told us about."

They ran to the village and found their way to Mary and Joseph. And there was the baby, lying in the manger. The shepherds told everyone what had happened and what the angel had said to them about this child. All who heard the shepherds' story expressed astonishment, but Mary quietly treasured these things in her heart and often thought about them.

Then the shepherds went back again to their fields and flocks, praising God for the visit of the angels, and because they had seen the child, just as the angel had told them.

Eight days later, at the baby's circumcision ceremony, he was named Jesus, the name given him by the angel before he was even conceived.

When the time came for Mary's purification offering at the Temple, as required by the laws of Moses after the birth of a child, his parents took him to Jerusalem to present him to the Lord; for in these laws God had said, "If a woman's first child is a boy, he shall be dedicated to the Lord."

At that time Jesus' parents also offered their sacrifice for purification—"either a pair of turtledoves or two young pigeons" was the legal requirement. That day a man named Simeon, a Jerusalem resident, was in the Temple. He was a good man, very devout, filled with the Holy Spirit and constantly expecting the Messiah to come soon. For the Holy Spirit had revealed to him that he would not die until he had seen him—God's anointed King. The Holy Spirit had impelled him to go to the Temple that day; and so, when Mary and Joseph arrived to present the baby Jesus to the Lord in obedience to the law, Simeon was there and took the child in his arms, praising God.

"Lord," he said, "now I can die content! For I have seen him as you promised me I would. I have seen the Savior you have given to the world. He is the Light that will shine upon the nations, and he will be the glory of your people Israel!"

Joseph and Mary just stood there, marveling at what was being said about Jesus.

Simeon blessed them but then said to Mary, "A sword shall pierce your soul, for this child shall be rejected by many in Israel, and this to their undoing. But he will be the greatest joy of many others. And the deepest thoughts of many hearts shall be revealed."

Anna, a prophetess, was also there in the Temple that day. She was the daughter of Phanuel, of the Jewish tribe of Asher, and was very old, for she had been a widow for eighty-four years following seven years of marriage. She never left the Temple but stayed there night and day, worshiping God by praying and often fasting.

She came along just as Simeon was talking with Mary and Joseph, and she also began thanking God and telling everyone in Jerusalem who had been awaiting the coming of the Savior that the Messiah had finally arrived.

When Jesus' parents had fulfilled all the requirements of the Law of God they returned home to Nazareth in Galilee. There the child became a strong, robust lad, and was known for wisdom beyond his years; and God poured out his blessings on him.

When Jesus was twelve years old he accompanied his parents to Jerusalem for the annual Passover Festival, which they attended each year. After the celebration was over they started home to Nazareth, but Jesus stayed behind in Jerusalem. His parents didn't miss him the first day, for they assumed he was with friends among the other travelers. But when he didn't show up that evening, they started to look for him among their relatives and friends; and when they couldn't find him, they went back to Jerusalem to search for him there.

Three days later they finally discovered him. He was in the Temple, sitting among the teachers of Law, discussing deep questions with them and amazing everyone with his understanding and answers.

His parents didn't know what to think. "Son!" his mother said to him. "Why have you done this to us? Your father and I have been frantic, searching for you everywhere."

"But why did you need to search?" he asked. "Didn't you realize that I would be here at the Temple, in my Father's House?" But they didn't understand what he meant.

Then he returned to Nazareth with them and was obedient to them; and his mother stored away all these things in her heart. So Jesus grew both tall and wise, and was loved by God and man.

CHAPTER THREE

A Voice Shouting

In THE FIFTEENTH YEAR of the reign of Emperor Tiberius Caesar, a message came from God to John (the son of Zacharias), as he was living out in the deserts. (Pilate was governor over Judea at that time; Herod, over Galilee; his brother Philip, over Iturea and Trachonitis; Lysanias, over Abilene; and Annas and Caiaphas were High Priests.) Then John went from place to place on both sides of the Jordan River, preaching that people should be baptized to show that they had turned to God and away from their sins, in order to be forgiven.

In the words of Isaiah the prophet, John was "a voice shouting from the barren wilderness, 'Prepare a road for the Lord to travel on! Widen the pathway before him! Level the mountains! Fill up the valleys! Straighten the curves! Smooth out the ruts! And then all mankind shall see the Savior sent from God.' "

Here is a sample of John's preaching to the crowds that came for baptism: "You brood of snakes! You are trying to escape hell without truly turning to God! That is why you want to be baptized! First go and prove by the way you live that you really have repented. And don't think you are safe because you are descendants of Abraham. That isn't enough. God can produce children of Abraham from these desert stones! The axe of his judgment is poised over you, ready to sever your roots and cut you down. Yes, every tree that does not produce good fruit will be chopped down and thrown into the fire."

The crowd replied, "What do you want us to do?"

"If you have two coats," he replied, "give one to the poor. If you have extra food, give it away to those who are hungry."

Even tax collectors—notorious for their corruption—came to be baptized and asked, "How shall we prove to you that we have abandoned our sins?"

"By your honesty," he replied. "Make sure you collect no more taxes than the Roman government requires you to."

"And us," asked some soldiers, "what about us?"

John replied, "Don't extort money by threats and violence; don't accuse anyone of what you know he didn't do; and be content with your pay!"

Everyone was expecting the Messiah to come soon, and eager to know whether or not John was he. This was the question of the hour, and was being discussed everywhere.

John answered the question by saying, "I baptize only with water; but someone is coming soon who has far higher authority than mine; in fact, I am not even worthy of being his slave. He will baptize you with fire—with the Holy Spirit. He will separate chaff from grain, and burn up the chaff with eternal fire and store away the grain." He used many such warnings as he announced the Good News to the people.

(But after John had publicly criticized Herod, governor of Galilee, for marrying Herodias, his brother's wife, and for many other wrongs he had done, Herod put John in prison, thus adding this sin to all his many others.) Then one day, after the crowds had been baptized, Jesus himself was baptized; and as he was praying, the heavens opened, and the Holy Spirit in the form of a dove settled upon him, and a voice from heaven said, "You are my much loved Son, yes, my delight."

Jesus was about thirty years old when he began his public ministry.

Jesus was known as the son of Joseph.

Joseph's father was Heli;
Heli's father was Matthat;
Matthat's father was Levi;
Levi's father was Melchi;
Melchi's father was Jannai;
Jannai's father was Joseph;
Joseph's father was Mattathias;
Mattathias' father was Amos;
Amos' father was Nahum;
Nahum's father was Esli;
Esli's father was Naggai;
Naggai's father was Maath;
Maath's father was Mattathias;
Mattathias' father was Semein;
Semein's father was Josech;
Josech's father was Joda;
Joda's father was Joanan;
Joanan's father was Rhesa;
Rhesa's father was Zerubbabel;
Zerubbabel's father was Shealtiel;
Shealtiel's father was Neri;
Neri's father was Melchi;
Melchi's father was Addi;
Addi's father was Cosam;
Cosam's father was Elmadam;
Elmadam's father was Er;
Er's father was Joshua;
Joshua's father was Eliezer;
Eliezer's father was Jorim;
Jorim's father was Matthat;
Matthat's father was Levi;
Levi's father was Simeon;

Simeon's father was Judah;
Judah's father was Joseph;
Joseph's father was Jonam;
Jonam's father was Eliakim;
Eliakim's father was Melea;
Melea's father was Menna;
Menna's father was Mattatha;
Mattatha's father was Nathan;
Nathan's father was David;
David's father was Jesse;
Jesse's father was Obed;
Obed's father was Boaz;
Boaz' father was Salmon;
Salmon's father was Nahshon;
Nahshon's father was Amminadab;
Amminadab's father was Admin;
Admin's father was Arni;
Arni's father was Hezron;
Hezron's father was Perez;
Perez' father was Judah;
Judah's father was Jacob;
Jacob's father was Isaac;
Isaac's father was Abraham;
Abraham's father was Terah;
Terah's father was Nahor;
Nahor's father was Serug;
Serug's father was Reu;
Reu's father was Peleg;
Peleg's father was Eber;
Eber's father was Shelah;
Shelah's father was Cainan;
Cainan's father was Arphaxad;
Arphaxad's father was Shem;
Shem's father was Noah;
Noah's father was Lamech;

Lamech's father was Methuselah;
Methuselah's father was Enoch;
Enoch's father was Jared;
Jared's father was Mahalaleel;
Mahalaleel's father was Cainan;
Cainan's father was Enos;
Enos' father was Seth;
Seth's father was Adam;
Adam's father was God.

CHAPTER FOUR

Demons

THEN JESUS, full of the Holy Spirit, left the Jordan River, being urged by the Spirit out into the barren wastelands of Judea, where Satan tempted him for forty days. He ate nothing all that time, and was very hungry.

Satan said, "If you are God's Son, tell this stone to become a loaf of bread."

But Jesus replied, "It is written in the Scriptures, 'Other things in life are much more important than bread!' "

Then Satan took him up and revealed to him all the kingdoms of the world in a moment of time; and the devil told him, "I will give you all these splendid kingdoms and their glory—for they are mine to give to anyone I wish—if you will only get down on your knees and worship me."

Jesus replied, "We must worship God, and him alone. So it is written in the Scriptures."

Then Satan took him to Jerusalem to a high roof of the Temple and said, "If you are the Son of God, jump off! For the Scriptures say that God will send his angels to guard you and to keep you from crashing to the pavement below!"

Jesus replied, "The Scriptures also say, 'Do not put the Lord your God to a foolish test.' "

When the devil had ended all the temptations, he left Jesus for a while and went away.

Then Jesus returned to Galilee, full of the Holy Spirit's power. Soon he became well known throughout all that region for his sermons in the synagogues; everyone praised him.

When he came to the village of Nazareth, his boyhood home, he went as usual to the synagogue on Saturday, and stood up to read the Scriptures. The book of Isaiah the prophet was handed to him, and he opened it to the place where it says:

"The Spirit of the Lord is upon me; he has appointed me to preach Good News to the poor· he has sent me to heal the brokenhearted and to announce that captives shall be released and the blind shall see, that the downtrodden shall be freed from their oppressors, and that God is ready to give blessings to all who come to him."

He closed the book and handed it back to the attendant and sat down, while everyone in the synagogue gazed at him intently. Then he added, "These Scriptures came true today!"

All who were there spoke well of him and were amazed by the beautiful words that fell from his lips. "How can this be?" they asked. "Isn't this Joseph's son?"

Then he said, "Probably you will quote me that proverb, 'Physician, heal yourself'—meaning, 'Why don't you do miracles here in your home town like those you did in Capernaum?' But I solemnly declare to you that no prophet is accepted in his own home town! For example, remember how Elijah the prophet used a miracle to help the widow of Zarephath—a foreigner from the land of Sidon. There were many Jewish widows needing help in those days of famine, for there had been no rain for three and one-half years, and hunger stalked the land; yet Elijah was not sent to them. Or think of the prophet Elisha, who healed Naaman, a Syrian, rather than the many Jewish lepers needing help."

These remarks stung them to fury; and jumping up, they mobbed him and took him to the edge of the hill on which the city was built, to push him over the cliff. But he walked away through the crowd and left them.

Then he returned to Capernaum, a city in Galilee, and preached there in the synagogue every Saturday. Here, too, the people were amazed at the things he said. For he spoke as one who knew the truth, instead of merely quoting the opinions of others as his authority.

Once as he was teaching in the synagogue, a man possessed by a demon began shouting at Jesus, "Go away! We want nothing to do with you, Jesus from Nazareth. You have come to destroy us. I know who you are—the Holy Son of God."

Jesus cut him short. "Be silent!" he told the demon. "Come out!" The demon threw the man to the floor as the crowd watched, and then left him without hurting him further.

Amazed, the people asked, "What is in this man's words that even demons obey him?" The story of what he had done spread like wildfire throughout the whole region.

After leaving the synagogue that day, he went to Simon's home where he found Simon's mother-in-law very sick with a high fever. "Please heal her," everyone begged.

Standing at her bedside he spoke to the fever, rebuking it, and immediately her temperature returned to normal and she got up and prepared a meal for them!

As the sun went down that evening, all the villagers who had any sick people in their homes, no matter what their diseases were, brought them to Jesus; and the touch of his hands healed every one! Some were possessed by demons; and the demons came out at his command, shouting, "You are the Son of God." But because they knew he was the Christ, he stopped them and told them to be silent.

Early the next morning he went out into the desert. The crowds searched everywhere for him and when they finally found him they begged him not to leave them, but to stay at

Capernaum. But he replied, "I must preach the Good News of the Kingdom of God in other places too, for that is why I was sent." So he continued to travel around preaching in synagogues throughout Judea.

CHAPTER FIVE

Two Empty Boats

ONE DAY as he was preaching on the shore of Lake Gennesaret, great crowds pressed in on him to listen to the Word of God. He noticed two empty boats standing at the water's edge while the fishermen washed their nets. Stepping into one of the boats, Jesus asked Simon, its owner, to push out a little into the water, so that he could sit in the boat and speak to the crowds from there.

When he had finished speaking, he said to Simon, "Now go out where it is deeper and let down your nets and you will catch a lot of fish!"

"Sir," Simon replied, "we worked hard all last night and didn't catch a thing. But if you say so, we'll try again."

And this time their nets were so full that they began to tear! A shout for help brought their partners in the other boat and soon both boats were filled with fish and on the verge of sinking.

When Simon Peter realized what had happened, he fell to his knees before Jesus and said, "Oh, sir, please leave us—I'm too much of a sinner for you to have around." For he was

awestruck by the size of their catch, as were the others with him, and his partners too—James and John, the sons of Zebedee. Jesus replied, "Don't be afraid! From now on you'll be fishing for the souls of men!"

And as soon as they landed, they left everything and went with him.

One day in a certain village he was visiting, there was a man with an advanced case of leprosy. When he saw Jesus he fell to the ground before him, face downward in the dust, begging to be healed.

"Sir," he said, "if you only will, you can clear me of every trace of my disease."

Jesus reached out and touched the man and said, "Of course I will. Be healed." And the leprosy left him instantly! Then Jesus instructed him to go at once without telling anyone what had happened and be examined by the Jewish priest. "Offer the sacrifice Moses' law requires for lepers who are healed," he said, "This will prove to everyone that you are well." Now the report of his power spread even faster and vast crowds came to hear him preach and to be healed of their diseases. But he often withdrew to the wilderness for prayer.

One day while he was teaching, some Jewish religious leaders and teachers of the Law were sitting nearby. (It seemed that these men showed up from every village in all Galilee and Judea, as well as from Jerusalem.) And the Lord's healing power was upon him.

Then—look! Some men came carrying a paralyzed man on a sleeping mat. They tried to push through the crowd to Jesus but couldn't reach him. So they went up on the roof above him, took off some tiles and lowered the sick man down into the crowd, still on his sleeping mat, right in front of Jesus.

Seeing their faith, Jesus said to the man, "My friend, your sins are forgiven!"

"Who does this fellow think he is?" the Pharisees and teachers of the Law exclaimed among themselves. "This is blasphemy! Who but God can forgive sins?"

Jesus knew what they were thinking, and he replied, "Why is it blasphemy? I, the Messiah, have the authority on earth to forgive sins. But talk is cheap—anybody could say that. So I'll prove it to you by healing this man." Then, turning to the paralyzed man, he commanded, "Pick up your stretcher and go on home, for you are healed!"

And immediately, as everyone watched, the man jumped to his feet, picked up his mat and went home praising God! Everyone present was gripped with awe and fear. And they praised God, remarking over and over again, "We have seen strange things today."

Later on as Jesus left the town he saw a tax collector—with the usual reputation for cheating—sitting at a tax collection booth. The man's name was Levi. Jesus said to him, "Come and be one of my disciples!" So Levi left everything, sprang up and went with him.

Soon Levi held a reception in his home with Jesus as the guest of honor. Many of Levi's fellow tax collectors and other guests were there.

But the Pharisees and teachers of the Law complained bitterly to Jesus' disciples about his eating with such notorious sinners.

Jesus answered them, "It is the sick who need a doctor, not those in good health. My purpose is to invite sinners to turn from their sins, not to spend my time with those who think themselves already good enough."

Their next complaint was that Jesus' disciples were feasting instead of fasting. "John the Baptist's disciples are constantly going without food, and praying," they declared, "and so do the disciples of the Pharisees. Why are yours wining and dining?"

Jesus asked, "Do happy men fast? Do wedding guests go hungry while celebrating with the groom? But the time will come when the bridegroom will be killed; then they won't want to eat."

Then Jesus used this illustration: "No one tears off a piece of a new garment to make a patch for an old one. Not only will the new garment be ruined, but the old garment will look worse with a new patch on it! And no one puts new wine into old wineskins, for the new wine bursts the old skins, ruining the skins and spilling the wine. New wine must be put into new wineskins. But no one after drinking the old wine seems to want the fresh and the new. 'The old ways are best,' they say."

CHAPTER SIX

The Inner Circle

ONE SABBATH as Jesus and his disciples were walking through some grainfields, they were breaking off the heads of wheat, rubbing off the husks in their hands and eating the grains.

But some Pharisees said, "That's illegal! Your disciples are harvesting grain, and it's against the Jewish law to work on the Sabbath."

Jesus replied, "Don't you read the Scriptures? Haven't you ever read what King David did when he and his men were hungry? He went into the Temple and took the shewbread, the special bread that was placed before the Lord, and ate it—illegal as this was—and shared it with others." And Jesus added, "I am master even of the Sabbath."

On another Sabbath he was in the synagogue teaching, and a man was present whose right hand was deformed. The teachers of the Law and the Pharisees watched closely to see whether he would heal the man that day, since it was the Sabbath. For they were eager to find some charge to bring against him.

How well he knew their thoughts! But he said to the man

with the deformed hand, "Come and stand here where everyone can see." So he did.

Then Jesus said to the Pharisees and teachers of the Law, "I have a question for you. Is it right to do good on the Sabbath day, or to do harm? To save life, or to destroy it?"

He looked around at them one by one and then said to the man, "Reach out your hand." And as he did, it became completely normal again. At this, the enemies of Jesus were wild with rage, and began to plot his murder.

One day soon afterward he went out into the mountains to pray, and prayed all night. At daybreak he called together his followers and chose twelve of them to be the inner circle of his disciples. (They were appointed as his "apostles," or "missionaries.") Here are their names:

Simon (he also called him Peter),
Andrew (Simon's brother),
James,
John,
Philip,
Bartholomew,
Matthew,
Thomas,
James (the son of Alphaeus),
Simon (a member of the Zealots, a subversive political
party),
Judas (son of James),
Judas Iscariot (who later betrayed him).

When they came down the slopes of the mountain, they stood with Jesus on a large, level area, surrounded by many of his followers who, in turn, were surrounded by the crowds. For people from all over Judea and from Jerusalem and from as far north as the seacoasts of Tyre and Sidon had come to hear him or to be healed. And he cast out many demons. Everyone was trying to touch him, for when they did healing power went out from him and they were cured.

Then he turned to his disciples and said, "What happiness there is for you who are poor, for the Kingdom of God is yours! What happiness there is for you who are now hungry, for you are going to be satisfied! What happiness there is for you who weep, for the time will come when you shall laugh with joy! What happiness it is when others hate you and exclude you and insult you and smear your name because you are mine! When that happens, rejoice! Yes, leap for joy! For you will have a great reward awaiting you in heaven. And you will be in good company—the ancient prophets were treated that way too!

"But, oh, the sorrows that await the rich. For they have their only happiness down here. They are fat and prosperous now, but a time of awful hunger is before them. Their careless laughter now means sorrow then. And what sadness is ahead for those praised by the crowds—for *false* prophets have *always* been praised.

"Listen, all of you. Love your *enemies*. Do *good* to those who *hate* you. Pray for the happiness of those who *curse* you; implore God's blessing on those who *hurt* you.

"If someone slaps you on one cheek, let him slap the other too! If someone demands your coat, give him your shirt besides. Give what you have to anyone who asks you for it; and when things are taken away from you, don't worry about getting them back. Treat others as you want them to treat you.

"Do you think you deserve credit for merely loving those who love you? Even the godless do that! And if you do good only to those who do you good—is that so wonderful? Even sinners do that much! And if you lend money only to those who can repay you, what good is that? Even the most wicked will lend to their own kind for full return!

"Love your *enemies!* Do good to *them!* Lend to *them!* And don't be concerned about the fact that they won't repay. Then your reward from heaven will be very great, and you will truly be acting as sons of God: for he is kind to the *unthankful* and to those who are *very wicked*.

"Try to show as much compassion as your Father does. Never criticize or condemn—or it will all come back on you. Go easy on others; then they will do the same for you. For if you give, you will get! Your gift will return to you in full and overflowing measure, pressed down, shaken together to make room for more, and running over. Whatever measure you use to give—large or small—will be used to measure what is given back to you."

Here are some of the story-illustrations Jesus used in his sermons: "What good is it for one blind man to lead another? He will fall into a ditch and pull the other down with him. How can a student know more than his teacher? But if he works hard, he may learn as much.

"And why quibble about the speck in someone else's eye—his little fault—when a board is in your own? How can you think of saying to him, 'Brother, let me help you get rid of that speck in your eye,' when you can't see past the board in yours? Hypocrite! First get rid of the board, and then perhaps you can see well enough to deal with his speck!

"A tree from good stock doesn't produce scrub fruit nor do trees from poor stock produce choice fruit. A tree is identified by the kind of fruit it produces. Figs never grow on thorns, or grapes on bramble bushes. A good man produces good deeds from a good heart. And an evil man produces evil deeds from his hidden wickedness. Whatever is in the heart overflows into speech.

"So why do you call me 'Lord' when you won't obey me? But all those who come and listen and obey me are like a man who builds a house on a strong foundation laid upon the underlying rock. When the floodwaters rise and break against the house, it stands firm, for it is strongly built.

"But those who listen and don't obey are like a man who builds a house without a foundation. When the floods sweep down against that house, it crumbles into a heap of ruins."

CHAPTER SEVEN

More Than a Prophet

WHEN JESUS HAD finished his sermon he went back into the city of Capernaum.

Just at that time the highly prized slave of a Roman army captain was sick and near death. When the captain heard about Jesus, he sent some respected Jewish elders to ask him to come and heal his slave. So they began pleading earnestly with Jesus to come with them and help the man. They told him what a wonderful person the captain was.

"If anyone deserves your help, it is he," they said, "for he loves the Jews and even paid personally to build us a synagogue!"

Jesus went with them; but just before arriving at the house, the captain sent some friends to say, "Sir, don't inconvenience yourself by coming to my home, for I am not worthy of any such honor or even to come and meet you. Just speak a word from where you are, and my servant boy will be healed! I know, because I am under the authority of my superior officers, and I have authority over my men. I only need to say 'Go!' and they go; or 'Come!' and they come; and to my slave, 'Do this or that,' and he does it. So just say, 'Be healed!' and my servant will be well again!"

Jesus was amazed. Turning to the crowd he said, "Never among all the Jews in Israel have I met a man with faith like this."

And when the captain's friends returned to his house, they found the slave completely healed.

Not long afterward Jesus went with his disciples to the village of Nain, with the usual great crowd at his heels. A funeral procession was coming out as he approached the village gate. The boy who had died was the only son of his widowed mother, and many mourners from the village were with her.

When the Lord saw her, his heart overflowed with sympathy. "Don't cry!" he said. Then he walked over to the coffin and touched it, and the bearers stopped. "Laddie," he said, "come back to life again."

Then the boy sat up and began to talk to those around him! And Jesus gave him back to his mother.

A great fear swept the crowd, and they exclaimed with praises to God, "A mighty prophet has risen among us," and, "We have seen the hand of God at work today."

The report of what he did that day raced from end to end of Judea and even out across the borders.

The disciples of John the Baptist soon heard of all that Jesus was doing. When they told John about it, he sent two of his disciples to Jesus to ask him, "Are you really the Messiah? Or shall we keep on looking for him?"

The two disciples found Jesus while he was curing many sick people of their various diseases—healing the lame and the blind and casting out evil spirits. When they asked him John's question, this was his reply: "Go back to John and tell him all you have seen and heard here today; how those who were blind can see. The lame are walking without a limp. The lepers are completely healed. The deaf can hear again. The dead come back to life. And the poor are hearing the Good News. And tell him,

'Blessed is the one who does not lose his faith in me.' "

After they left, Jesus talked to the crowd about John. "Who is this man you went out into the Judean wilderness to see?" he asked. "Did you find him weak as grass, moved by every breath of wind? Did you find him dressed in expensive clothes? No! Men who live in luxury are found in palaces, not out in the wilderness. But did you find a prophet? Yes! And more than a prophet. He is the one to whom the Scriptures refer when they say, 'Look! I am sending my messenger ahead of you, to prepare the way before you.' In all humanity there is no one greater than John. And yet the least citizen of the Kingdom of God is greater than he."

And all who heard John preach—even the most wicked of them—agreed that God's requirements were right, and they were baptized by him. All, that is, except the Pharisees and teachers of Moses' Law. They rejected God's plan for them and refused John's baptism.

"What can I say about such men?" Jesus asked. "With what shall I compare them? They are like a group of children who complain to their friends, 'You don't like it if we play "wedding" and you don't like it if we play "funeral" '! For John the Baptist used to go without food and never took a drop of liquor all his life, and you said, 'He must be crazy!' But I eat my food and drink my wine, and you say, 'What a glutton Jesus is! And he drinks! And has the lowest sort of friends!' But I am sure you can always justify your inconsistencies."

One of the Pharisees asked Jesus to come to his home for lunch and Jesus accepted the invitation. As they sat down to eat, a woman of the streets—a prostitute—heard he was there and brought an exquisite flask filled with expensive perfume. Going in, she knelt behind him at his feet, weeping, with her tears falling down upon his feet; and she wiped them off with her hair and kissed them and poured the perfume on them.

When Jesus' host, a Pharisee, saw what was happening and who the woman was, he said to himself, "This proves that Jesus is no prophet, for if God had really sent him, he would know what kind of woman this one is!"

Then Jesus spoke up and answered his thoughts. "Simon," he said to the Pharisee, "I have something to say to you."

"All right, Teacher," Simon replied, "go ahead."

Then Jesus told him this story: "A man loaned money to two people—$5,000 to one and $500 to the other. But neither of them could pay him back, so he kindly forgave them both, letting them keep the money! Which do you suppose loved him most after that?"

"I suppose the one who had owed him the most," Simon answered.

"Correct," Jesus agreed.

Then he turned to the woman and said to Simon, "Look! See this woman kneeling here! When I entered your home, you didn't bother to offer me water to wash the dust from my feet, but she has washed them with her tears and wiped them with her hair. You refused me the customary kiss of greeting, but she has kissed my feet again and again from the time I first came in. You neglected the usual courtesy of olive oil to anoint my head, but she has covered my feet with rare perfume. Therefore her sins—and they are many—are forgiven, for she loved me much; but one who is forgiven little, shows little love."

And he said to her, "Your sins are forgiven."

Then the men at the table said to themselves, "Who does this man think he is, going around forgiving sins?"

And Jesus said to the woman, "Your faith has saved you; go in peace."

CHAPTER EIGHT

A Deep Wave of Fear

NOT LONG AFTERWARD he began a tour of the cities and villages of Galilee to announce the coming of the Kingdom of God, and took his twelve disciples with him. Some women went along, from whom he had cast out demons or whom he had healed; among them were Mary Magdalene (Jesus had cast out seven demons from her), Joanna, Chuza's wife (Chuza was King Herod's business manager and was in charge of his palace and domestic affairs), Susanna, and many others who were contributing from their private means to the support of Jesus and his disciples.

One day he gave this illustration to a large crowd that was gathering to hear him—while many others were still on the way, coming from other towns.

"A farmer went out to his field to sow grain. As he scattered the seed on the ground, some of it fell on a footpath and was trampled on; and the birds came and ate it as it lay exposed. Other seed fell on shallow soil with rock beneath. This seed began to grow, but soon withered and died for lack of moisture. Other seed landed in thistle patches, and the young grain stalks were soon choked out. Still other fell on fertile soil; this seed grew and produced a crop one hundred times as large as he had planted." (As he was giving this illustration he said, "If anyone has listening ears, use them now!")

His apostles asked him what the story meant.

He replied, "God has granted you to know the meaning of these parables, for they tell a great deal about the Kingdom of God. But these crowds hear the words and do not understand, just as the ancient prophets predicted.

"This is its meaning: The seed is God's message to men. The hard path where some seed fell represents the hard hearts of those who hear the words of God, but then the devil comes and steals the words away and prevents people from believing and being saved. The stony ground represents those who enjoy listening to sermons, but somehow the message never really gets through to them and doesn't take root and grow. They know the message is true, and sort of believe for a while; but when the hot winds of persecution blow, they lose interest. The seed among the thorns represents those who listen and believe God's words but whose faith afterward is choked out by worry and riches and the responsibilities and pleasures of life. And so they are never able to help anyone else to believe the Good News.

"But the good soil represents honest, good-hearted people. They listen to God's words and cling to them and steadily spread them to others who also soon believe."

Another time he asked, "Who ever heard of someone lighting a lamp and then covering it up to keep it from shining? No, lamps are mounted in the open where they can be seen. This illustrates the fact that someday everything in men's hearts shall be brought to light and made plain to all. So be careful how you listen; for whoever has, to him shall be given more; and whoever does not have, even what he thinks he has shall be taken away from him."

Once when his mother and brothers came to see him, they couldn't get into the house where he was teaching, because of the crowds. When Jesus heard they were standing outside and wanted to see him, he remarked, "My mother and my brothers are all those who hear the message of God and obey it."

One day about that time, as he and his disciples were out in a boat, he suggested that they cross to the other side of the lake. On the way across he lay down for a nap, and while he was sleeping the wind began to rise. A fierce storm developed that threatened to swamp them, and they were in real danger.

They rushed over and woke him up. "Master, Master, we are sinking!" they screamed.

So he spoke to the storm: "Quiet down," he said, and the wind and waves subsided and all was calm! Then he asked them, "Where is your faith?"

And they were filled with awe and fear of him and said to one another, "Who is this man, that even the winds and waves obey him?"

So they arrived at the other side, in the Gerasene country across the lake from Galilee. As he was climbing out of the boat a man from the city of Gadara came to meet him, a man who had been demon-possessed for a long time. Homeless and naked, he lived in a cemetery among the tombs. As soon as he saw Jesus he shrieked and fell to the ground before him, screaming, "What do you want with me, Jesus, Son of God Most High? Please, I beg you, oh, don't torment me!"

For Jesus was already commanding the demon to leave him. This demon had often taken control of the man so that even when shackled with chains he simply broke them and rushed out into the desert, completely under the demon's power. "What is your name?" Jesus asked the demon. "Legion," they replied—for the man was filled with thousands of them! They kept begging Jesus not to order them into the Bottomless Pit.

A herd of pigs was feeding on the mountainside nearby, and the demons pled with him to let them enter into the pigs. And Jesus said they could. So they left the man and went into the pigs, and immediately the whole herd rushed down the mountainside and fell over a cliff into the lake below, where they drowned. The herdsmen rushed away to the nearby city, spreading the news as they ran.

Soon a crowd came out to see for themselves what had happened and saw the man who had been demon-possessed sitting quietly at Jesus' feet, clothed and sane! And the whole crowd was badly frightened. Then those who had seen it happen told how the demon-possessed man had been healed. And everyone begged Jesus to go away and leave them alone (for a deep wave of fear had swept over them). So he returned to the boat and left, crossing back to the other side of the lake.

The man who had been demon-possessed begged to go too, but Jesus said no.

"Go back to your family," he told him, "and tell them what a wonderful thing God has done for you."

So he went all through the city telling everyone about Jesus' mighty miracle.

On the other side of the lake the crowds received him with open arms, for they had been waiting for him.

And now a man named Jairus, a leader of a Jewish synagogue, came and fell down at Jesus' feet and begged him to come home with him, for his only child was dying, a little girl twelve years old. Jesus went with him, pushing through the crowds.

As they went a woman who wanted to be healed came up behind and touched him, for she had been slowly bleeding for twelve years, and could find no cure (though she had spent everything she had on doctors). But the instant she touched the edge of his robe, the bleeding stopped.

"Who touched me?" Jesus asked.

Everyone denied it, and Peter said, "Master, so many are crowding against you. . . ."

But Jesus told him, "No, it was someone who deliberately touched me, for I felt healing power go out from me."

When the woman realized that Jesus knew, she began to

tremble and fell to her knees before him and told why she had touched him and that now she was well.

"Daughter," he said to her, "your faith has healed you. Go in peace."

While he was still speaking to her, a messenger arrived from the Jairus' home with the news that the little girl was dead. "She's gone," he told her father; "there's no use troubling the Teacher now."

But when Jesus heard what had happened, he said to the father, "Don't be afraid! Just trust me, and she'll be all right."

When they arrived at the house Jesus wouldn't let anyone into the room except Peter, James, John, and the little girl's father and mother. The home was filled with mourning people, but he said, "Stop the weeping! She isn't dead; she is only asleep!" This brought scoffing and laughter, for they all knew she was dead.

Then he took her by the hand and called, "Get up, little girl!" And at that moment her life returned and she jumped up! "Give her something to eat!" he said. Her parents were overcome with happiness, but Jesus insisted that they not tell anyone the details of what had happened.

CHAPTER NINE

With an Iron Will

ONE DAY JESUS called together his twelve apostles and gave them authority over all demons — power to cast them out — and to heal all diseases. Then he sent them away to tell everyone about the coming of the Kingdom of God and to heal the sick.

"Don't even take along a walking stick," he instructed them, "nor a beggar's bag, nor food, nor money. Not even an extra coat. Be a guest in only one home at each village.

"If the people of a town won't listen to you when you enter it, turn around and leave, demonstrating God's anger against it by shaking its dust from your feet as you go."

So they began their circuit of the villages, preaching the Good News and healing the sick.

When reports of Jesus' miracles reached Herod, the governor, he was worried and puzzled, for some were saying, "This is John the Baptist come back to life again"; and others, "It is Elijah or some other ancient prophet risen from the dead." These rumors were circulating all over the land.

"I beheaded John," Herod said, "so who is this man about

whom I hear such strange stories?" And he tried to see him.

After the apostles returned to Jesus and reported what they had done, he slipped quietly away with them toward the city of Bethsaida. But the crowds found out where he was going, and followed. And he welcomed them, teaching them again about the Kingdom of God and curing those who were ill.

Late in the afternoon all twelve of the disciples came and urged him to send the people away to the nearby villages and farms, to find food and lodging for the night. "For there is nothing to eat here in this deserted spot," they said.

But Jesus replied, "You feed them!"

"Why, we have only five loaves of bread and two fish among the lot of us," they protested; "or are you expecting us to go and buy enough for this whole mob?" For there were about 5,000 men there!

"Just tell them to sit down on the ground in groups of about fifty each," Jesus replied. So they did.

Jesus took the five loaves and two fish and looked up into the sky and gave thanks; then he broke off pieces for his disciples to set before the crowd. And everyone ate and ate; still, twelve basketfulls of scraps were picked up afterward!

One day as he was alone, praying, with his disciples nearby, he came over and asked them, "Who are the people saying I am?"

"John the Baptist," they told him, "or perhaps Elijah or one of the other ancient prophets risen from the dead."

Then he asked them, "Who do you think I am?"

Peter replied, "The Messiah — the Christ of God!"

He gave them strict order not to speak of this to anyone. "For I, the Messiah, must suffer much," he said, "and be rejected by the Jewish leaders — the elders, chief priests, and teachers of the Law — and be killed; and three days later I will come back to life again!"

Then he said to all, "Anyone who wants to follow me must put aside his own desires and conveniences and carry his cross with him every day and keep close to me! Whoever loses his life for my sake will save it, but whoever insists on keeping his life will lose it; and what profit is there in gaining the whole world when it means forfeiting one's self?

"When I, the Messiah, come in my glory and in the glory of the Father and the holy angels, I will be ashamed then of all who are ashamed of me and of my words now. But this is the simple truth — some of you who are standing here right now will not die until you have seen the Kingdom of God."

Eight days later he took Peter, James, and John with him into the hills to pray.

And as he was praying, his face began to shine, and his clothes became dazzling white and blazed with light. Then two men appeared and began talking with him — Moses and Elijah! They were splendid in appearance, glorious to see; and they were speaking of his death at Jerusalem, to be carried out in accordance with God's plan.

"Peter and the others had been very drowsy and had fallen asleep. Now they woke up and saw Jesus covered with brightness and glory, and the two men standing with him. As Moses and Elijah were starting to leave, Peter, all confused and not even knowing what he was saying, blurted out, "Master, this is wonderful! We'll put up three shelters — one for you and one for Moses and one for Elijah!"

But even as he was saying this, a bright cloud formed above them; and terror gripped them as it covered them. And a voice from the cloud said, "This is my Son, my Chosen One; listen to him."

Then, as the voice died away, Jesus was there alone with his disciples. They didn't tell anyone what they had seen until long afterward.

"The next day as they descended from the hill, a huge crowd met him, and a man in the crowd called out to him, "Teacher, this boy here is my only son, and a demon keeps seizing him, making him scream; and it throws him into convulsions so that he foams at the mouth; it is always hitting him and hardly ever leaves him alone. I begged your disciples to cast the demon out, but they couldn't."

"O you stubborn faithless people," Jesus said to his disciples, "how long should I put up with you? Bring him here."

As the boy was coming the demon knocked him to the ground and threw him into a violent convulsion. But Jesus ordered the demon to come out, and healed the boy and handed him over to his father.

Awe gripped the people as they saw this display of the power of God.

Meanwhile, as they were exclaiming over all the wonderful things he was doing, Jesus said to his disciples, "Listen to me and remember what I say: I, the Messiah, am going to be betrayed." But the disciples didn't know what he meant, for their minds had been sealed and they were afraid to ask him.

Now came an argument among them as to which of them would be greatest in the coming Kingdom! But Jesus knew their thoughts, so he stood a little child beside him and said to them, "Anyone who takes care of a little child like this is caring for me! And whoever cares for me is caring for God who sent me. Your care for others is the measure of your greatness." His disciple John came to him and said, "Master, we saw someone using your name to cast out demons. And we told him not to. After all, he isn't in our group."

But Jesus said, "You shouldn't have done that! For anyone who is not against you is for you."

As the time drew near for his return to heaven, he moved steadily onward toward Jerusalem with an iron will.

One day he sent messengers ahead to reserve rooms for them in a Samaritan village. But they were turned away! The people of the village refused to have anything to do with them because they were headed for Jerusalem.

When word came back of what had happened, James and John said to Jesus, "Master, shall we order fire down from heaven to burn them up?" But Jesus turned and rebuked them, and they went on to another village.

As they were walking along, someone said to Jesus, "I will always follow you no matter where you go."

But Jesus replied, "Remember, I don't even own a place to lay my head. Foxes have dens to live in, and birds have nests, but I, the Messiah, have no earthly home at all."

Another time, when he invited a man to come with him to be his disciple, the man agreed — but wanted to wait until his father's death.

Jesus replied, "Let those without eternal life concern themselves with things like that. Your duty is to come and preach the coming of the Kingdom of God to all the world."

Another said, "Yes, Lord, I will come, but first let me ask permission of those at home."

But Jesus told him, "Anyone who lets himself be distracted from the work I plan for him is not fit for the Kingdom of God."

CHAPTER TEN

The Agent

THE LORD NOW CHOSE seventy other disciples and sent them on ahead in pairs to all the towns and villages he planned to visit later.

These were his instructions to them: "Plead with the Lord of the harvest to send out more laborers to help you, for the harvest is so plentiful and the workers so few. Go now, and remember that I am sending you out as lambs among wolves. Don't take any money with you, or a beggar's bag, or even an extra pair of shoes. And don't waste time along the way.

"Whenever you enter a home, give it your blessing. If it is worthy of the blessing, the blessing will stand; if not, the blessing will return to you.

"When you enter a village, don't shift around from home to home, but stay in one place, eating and drinking without question whatever is set before you. And don't hesitate to accept hospitality, for the workman is worthy of his wages!

"If a town welcomes you, follow these two rules: (1) Eat whatever is set before you. (2) Heal the sick; and as you heal them, say, 'The Kingdom of God is very near you now.'

44

"But if a town refuses you, go out into its streets and say, 'We wipe the dust of your town from our feet as a public announcement of your doom. Never forget how close you were to the Kingdom of God!' Even wicked Sodom will be better off than such a city on the Judgment Day. What horrors await you, you cities of Chorazin and Bethsaida! For if the miracles I did for you had been done in the cities of Tyre and Sidon, their people would have sat in deep repentance long ago, clothed in sackcloth and throwing ashes on their heads to show their remorse. Yes, Tyre and Sidon will receive less punishment on the Judgment Day than you. And you people of Capernaum, what shall I say about you? Will you be exalted to heaven? No, you shall be brought down to hell."

Then he said to the disciples, "Those who welcome you are welcoming me. And those who reject you are rejecting me. And those who reject me are rejecting God, who sent me."

When the seventy disciples returned, they joyfully reported to him, "Even the demons obey us when we use your name."

"Yes," he told them, "I saw Satan falling from heaven as a flash of lightning! And I have given you authority over all the power of the Enemy, and to walk among serpents and scorpions and to crush them. Nothing shall injure you! However, the important thing is not that demons obey you, but that your names are registered as citizens of heaven."

Then he was filled with the joy of the Holy Spirit and said, "I praise you, O Father, Lord of heaven and earth, for hiding these things from the intellectuals and worldly wise and for revealing them to those who are as trusting as little children. Yes, thank you, Father, for that is the way you wanted it. I am the Agent of my Father in everything; and no one really knows the Son except the Father, and no one really knows the Father except the Son and those to whom the Son chooses to reveal him."

Then, turning to the twelve disciples, he said quietly, "How privileged you are to see what you have seen. Many a prophet and king of old has longed for these days, to see and hear what you have seen and heard!"

One day an expert on Moses' laws came to test Jesus' orthodoxy by asking him this question: "Teacher, what does a man need to do to live forever in heaven?"

Jesus replied, "What does Moses' law say about it?"

"It says," he replied, "that you must love the Lord your God with all your heart, and with all your soul, and with all your strength, and with all your mind. And you must love your neighbor just as much as you love yourself."

"Right!" Jesus told him. "*Do* this and *you* shall live!"

The man wanted to justify his lack of love for some kinds of people, so he asked, "Which neighbors?"

Jesus replied with an illustration: "A Jew going on a trip from Jerusalem to Jericho was attacked by bandits. They stripped him of his clothes and money and beat him up and left him lying half dead beside the road.

"By chance a Jewish priest came along; and when he saw the man lying there, he crossed to the other side of the road and passed him by. A Jewish Temple-assistant walked over and looked at him lying there, but then went on.

"But a despised Samaritan came along, and when he saw him, he felt deep pity. Kneeling beside him the Samaritan soothed his wounds with medicine and bandaged them. Then he put the man on his donkey and walked along beside him till they came to an inn, where he nursed him through the night. The next day he handed the innkeeper two twenty-dollar bills and told him to take care of the man. 'If his bill runs higher than that,' he said, 'I'll pay the difference the next time I am here.'

"Now which of these three would you say was a neighbor to the bandits' victim?"

The man replied, "The one who showed him some pity."

Then Jesus said, "Yes, now go and do the same."

As Jesus and the disciples continued on their way to Jerusalem they came to a village where a woman named Martha welcomed them into her home. Her sister Mary sat on the floor, listening to Jesus as he talked.

But Martha was the jittery type, and was worrying over the big dinner she was preparing.

She came to Jesus and said, "Sir, doesn't it seem unfair to you that my sister just sits here while I do all the work? Tell her to come and help me."

But the Lord said to her, "Martha, dear friend, you are so upset over all these details! There is really only one thing worth being concerned about. Mary has discovered it—and I won't take it away from her!"

CHAPTER ELEVEN

Seats of Honor

ONCE WHEN JESUS had been out praying, one of his disciples came to him as he finished and said, "Lord, teach us a prayer to recite just as John taught one to his disciples."

And this is the prayer he taught them: "Father, may your name be honored for its holiness; send your Kingdom soon. Give us our food day by day. And forgive our sins—for we have forgiven those who sinned against us. And don't allow us to be tempted."

Then, teaching them more about prayer, he used this illustration: "Suppose you went to a friend's house at midnight, wanting to borrow three loaves of bread. You would shout up to him, 'A friend of mine has just arrived for a visit and I've nothing to give him to eat.' He would call down from his bedroom, 'Please don't ask me to get up. The door is locked for the night and we are all in bed. I just can't help you this time.'

"But I'll tell you this—though he won't do it as a friend, if you keep knocking long enough he will get up and give you everything you want—just because of your persistence. And so it is with prayer—keep on asking and you will keep on getting;

keep on looking and you will keep on finding; knock and the door will be opened. Everyone who asks, receives; all who seek, find; and the door is opened to everyone who knocks.

"You men who are fathers—if your boy asks for bread, do you give him a stone? If he asks for fish, do you give him a snake? If he asks for an egg, do you give him a scorpion? Of course not!

"And if even sinful persons like yourselves give children what they need, don't you realize that your heavenly Father will do at least as much, and give the Holy Spirit to those who ask for him?"

Once, when Jesus cast out a demon from a man who couldn't speak, his voice returned to him. The crowd was excited and enthusiastic, but some said, "No wonder he can cast them out. He gets his power from Satan, the king of demons!" Others asked for something to happen in the sky to prove his claim of being the Messiah.

He knew the thoughts of each of them, so he said, "Any kingdom filled with civil war is doomed; so is a home filled with argument and strife. Therefore, if what you say is true, that Satan is fighting against himself by empowering me to cast out his demons, how can his kingdom survive? And if I am empowered by Satan, what about your own followers? For they cast out demons! Do you think this proves they are possessed by Satan? Ask *them* if you are right! But if I am casting out demons because of power from God, it proves that the Kingdom of God has arrived.

"For when Satan, strong and fully armed, guards his palace, it is safe—until someone stronger and better-armed attacks and overcomes him and strips him of his weapons and carries off his belongings.

"Anyone who is not for me is against me; if he isn't helping me, he is hurting my cause.

"When a demon is cast out of a man, it goes to the deserts, searching there for rest; but finding none, it returns to the person it left, and finds that its former home is all swept and clean. Then it goes and gets seven other demons more evil than itself, and they all enter the man. And so the poor fellow is seven times worse off than he was before."

As he was speaking, a woman in the crowd called out, "God bless your mother—the womb from which you came, and the breasts that gave you suck!"

He replied, "Yes, but even more blessed are all who hear the Word of God and put it into practice."

As the crowd pressed in upon him, he preached them this sermon: "These are evil times, with evil people. They keep asking for some strange happening in the skies to prove I am the Messiah, but the only proof I will give them is a miracle like that of Jonah, whose experiences proved to the people of Nineveh that God had sent him. My similar experience will prove that God has sent me to these people.

"And at the Judgment Day the Queen of Sheba shall arise and point her finger at this generation, condemning it, for she went on a long, hard journey to listen to the wisdom of Solomon; but one far greater than Solomon is here and few pay any attention.

"The men of Nineveh, too, shall arise and condemn this nation, for they repented at the preaching of Jonah; and someone far greater than Jonah is here but this nation won't listen.

"No one lights a lamp and hides it! Instead, he puts it on a lampstand to give light to all who enter the room. Your eyes light up your inward being. A pure eye lets sunshine into your soul. A lustful eye shuts out the light and plunges you into darkness. So watch out that the sunshine isn't blotted out. If you are filled with light within, with no dark corners, then your face will be radiant too, as though a floodlight is beamed upon you."

As he was speaking, one of the Pharisees asked him home for a meal. When Jesus arrived, he sat down to eat without first performing the ceremonial washing required by Jewish custom.

This greatly surprised his host.

Then Jesus said to him, "You Pharisees wash the outside, but inside you are still dirty—full of greed and wickedness! Fools! Didn't God make the inside as well as the outside? Purity is best demonstrated by generosity.

"But woe to you Pharisees! For though you are careful to tithe even the smallest part of your income, you completely forget about justice and the love of God. You should tithe, yes, but you should not leave these other things undone.

"Woe to you Pharisees! For how you love the seats of honor in the synagogues and the respectful greetings from everyone as you walk through the markets! Yes, awesome judgment is awaiting you. For you are like hidden graves in a field. Men go by you with no knowledge of the corruption they are passing."

"Sir," said an expert in religious law who was standing there, "you have insulted my profession, too, in what you just said."

"Yes," said Jesus, "the same horrors await you! For you crush people beneath impossible religious demands—demands that you yourselves would never think of trying to keep. Woe to you! For you are exactly like your ancestors who killed the prophets long ago. Murderers! You agree with your fathers that what they did was right—you would have done the same yourselves.

"This is what God says about you: 'I will send prophets and apostles to you, and you will kill some of them and chase away the others.'

"And you of this generation will be held responsible for the murder of God's servants from the founding of the world—from the murder of Abel to the murder of Zechariah who perished between the altar and the sanctuary. Yes, it will surely be charged against you.

"Woe to you experts in religion! For you hide the truth from the people. You won't accept it for yourselves, and you prevent others from having a chance to believe it."

The Pharisees and legal experts were furious; and from that

time on they plied him fiercely with a host of questions, trying to trap him into saying something for which they could have him arrested.

CHAPTER TWELVE

Warnings

MEANWHILE THE CROWDS grew until thousands upon thousands were milling about and crushing each other. He turned now to his disciples and warned them, "More than anything else, beware of these Pharisees and the way they pretend to be good when they aren't. But such hypocrisy cannot be hidden forever. It will become as evident as yeast in dough. Whatever they have said in the dark shall be heard in the light, and what you have whispered in the inner rooms shall be broadcast from the housetops for all to hear!

"Dear friends, don't be afraid of these who want to murder you. They can only kill the body; they have no power over your souls. But I'll tell you whom to fear—fear God, who has the power to kill and then cast into hell.

"What is the price of five sparrows? A couple of pennies? Not much more than that. Yet God does not forget a single one of them. And he knows the number of hairs on your head! Never fear, you are far more valuable to him than a whole flock of sparrows.

"And I assure you of this: I, the Messiah, will publicly honor you in the presence of God's angels if you publicly acknowledge me here on earth as your Friend. But I will deny before the angels those who deny me here among men. (Yet those who speak against me may be forgiven—while those who speak against the Holy Spirit shall never be forgiven.)

"And when you are brought to trial before these Jewish rulers and authorities in the synagogues, don't be concerned about what to say in your defense, for the Holy Spirit will give you the right words even as you are standing there."

Then someone called from the crowd, "Sir, please tell my brother to divide my father's estate with me."

But Jesus replied, "Man, who made me a judge over you to decide such things as that? Beware! Don't always be wishing for what you don't have. For real life and real living are not related to how rich we are."

Then he gave an illustration: "A rich man had a fertile farm that produced fine crops. In fact, his barns were full to overflowing—he couldn't get everything in. He thought about his problem, and finally exclaimed, 'I know—I'll tear down my barns and build bigger ones! Then I'll have room enough. And I'll sit back and say to myself, "Friend, you have enough stored away for years to come. Now take it easy! Wine, women, and song for you!"'

"But God said to him, 'Fool! Tonight you die. Then who will get it all?'

"Yes, anyone is a fool who gets rich on earth but not in heaven."

Then turning to his disciples he said, "Don't worry about whether you have enough food to eat or clothes to wear. For life consists of far more than food and clothes. Look at the ravens—they don't plant or harvest or have barns to store away their food, and yet they get along all right—for God feeds them. And you are far more valuable to him than any birds!

"And besides, what's the use of worrying? What good does it do? Will it add a single day to your life? Of course not! And if worry can't even do such little things as that, what's the use of worrying over bigger things?

"Look at the lilies! They don't toil and spin, and yet Solomon in all his glory was not robed as well as they are. And if God provides clothing for the flowers that are here today and gone tomorrow, don't you suppose that he will provide clothing for you, you doubters? And don't worry about food—what to eat and drink; don't worry at all that God will provide it for you. All mankind scratches for its daily bread, but your heavenly Father knows your needs. He will always give you all you need from day to day if you will make the Kingdom of God your primary concern.

"So don't be afraid, little flock. For it gives your Father great happiness to give you the Kingdom. Sell what you have and give to those in need. This will fatten your purses in heaven! And the purses of heaven have no rips or holes in them. Your treasures there will never disappear; no thief can steal them; no moth can destroy them. Wherever your treasure is, there your heart and thoughts will also be.

"Be prepared—all dressed and ready—for your Lord's return from the wedding feast. Then you will be ready to open the door and let him in the moment he arrives and knocks. There will be great joy for those who are ready and waiting for his return. He himself will seat them and put on a waiter's uniform and serve them as they sit and eat! He may come at nine o'clock at night—or even at midnight. But whenever he comes there will be joy for his servants who are ready!

"Each of you would be ready for him if you knew the exact hour of his return—just as you would be ready for a thief if you knew when he was coming. So be ready all the time. For I, the Messiah, will come when least expected."

Peter asked, "Lord, are you talking just to us or to everyone?"

And the Lord replied, "I'm talking to any faithful, sensible man whose master gives him the responsibility of feeding the other servants. If his master returns and finds that he has done a good job, there will be a reward—his master will put him in charge of all he owns.

"But if the man begins to think, 'My Lord won't be back for a long time,' and begins to whip the men and women he is supposed to protect, and to spend his time at drinking parties and in drunkenness—well, his master will return without notice and remove him from his position of trust and assign him to the place of the unfaithful. He will be severely punished, for though he knew his duty he refused to do it.

"But anyone who is not aware that he is doing wrong will be punished only lightly. Much is required from those to whom much is given, for their responsibility is greater.

"I have come to bring fire to the earth, and, oh, that my task were completed! There is a terrible baptism ahead of me, and how I am pent up until it is accomplished!

"Do you think I have come to give peace to the earth? *No!* Rather, strife and division! From now on families will be split apart, three in favor of me, and two against—or perhaps the other way around. A father will decide one way about me; his son, the other; mother and daughter will disagree; and the decision of an honored mother-in-law will be spurned by her daughter-in-law."

Then he turned to the crowd and said, "When you see clouds beginning to form in the west, you say, 'Here comes a shower.' And you are right.

"When the south wind blows you say, 'Today will be a scorcher.' And it is. Hypocrites! You interpret the sky well enough, but you refuse to notice the warnings all around you about the crisis ahead. Why do you refuse to see for yourselves what is right?

"If you meet your accuser on the way to court, try to settle the matter before it reaches the judge, lest he sentence you to jail; for if that happens you won't be free again until the last penny is paid in full."

CHAPTER THIRTEEN

The Kingdom

ABOUT THIS TIME Jesus was informed that Pilate had butchered some Jews from Galilee as they were sacrificing at the Temple in Jerusalem.

"Do you think they were worse sinners than other men from Galilee?" he asked. "Is that why they suffered? Not at all! And don't you realize that you also will perish unless you leave your evil ways and turn to God?

"And what about the eighteen men who died when the Tower of Siloam fell on them? Were they the worst sinners in Jerusalem? Not at all! And you, too, will perish unless you repent."

Then he used this illustration: "A man planted a fig tree in his garden and came again and again to see if he could find any fruit on it, but he was always disappointed. Finally he told his gardener to cut it down. 'I've waited three years and there hasn't been a single fig!' he said. 'Why bother with it any longer? It's taking up space we can use for something else.'

" 'Give it one more chance,' the gardener answered. 'Leave it another year, and I'll give it special attention and plenty of fertilizer. If we get figs next year, fine; if not, I'll cut it down.' "

One Sabbath as he was teaching in a synagogue, he saw a seriously handicapped woman who had been bent double for eighteen years and was unable to straighten herself.

Calling her over to him Jesus said, "Woman, you are healed of your sickness!" He touched her, and instantly she could stand straight. How she praised and thanked God!

But the local Jewish leader in charge of the synagogue was very angry about it because Jesus had healed her on the Sabbath day. "There are six days of the week to work," he shouted to the crowd. "Those are the days to come for healing, not on the Sabbath!"

But the Lord replied, "You hypocrite! You work on the Sabbath! Don't you untie your cattle from their stalls on the Sabbath and lead them out for water? And is it wrong for me, just because it is the Sabbath day, to free this Jewish woman from the bondage in which Satan has held her for eighteen years?"

This shamed his enemies. And all the people rejoiced at the wonderful things he did.

Now he began teaching them again about the Kingdom of God: "What is the Kingdom like?" he asked. "How can I illustrate it? It is like a tiny mustard seed planted in a garden; soon it grows into a tall bush, and the birds live among its branches. It is like yeast kneaded into dough, which works unseen until it has risen high and light."

He went from city to city and village to village, teaching as he went, always pressing onward toward Jerusalem.

Someone asked him, "Will only a few be saved?"

And he replied, "The door to heaven is narrow. Work hard to get in, for the truth is that many will try to enter but when the head of the house has locked the door, it will be too late. Then if you stand outside knocking, and pleading, 'Lord, open the door for us,' he will reply, 'I do not know you.'

" 'But we ate with you, and you taught in our streets,' you will say.

"And he will reply, 'I tell you, I don't know you. You can't come in here, guilty as you are. Go away.'

"And there will be great weeping and gnashing of teeth as you stand outside and see Abraham, Isaac, Jacob, and all the prophets within the Kingdom of God—for people will come from all over the world to take their places there. And note this: some who are despised now will be greatly honored then; and some who are highly thought of now will be least important then."

A few minutes later some Pharisees said to him, "Get out of here if you want to live, for King Herod is after you!"

Jesus replied, "Go tell that fox that I will keep on casting out demons and doing miracles of healing today and tomorrow; and the third day I will reach my destination. Yes, today, tomorrow, and the next day! For it wouldn't do for a prophet of God to be killed except in Jerusalem.

"O Jerusalem, Jerusalem! The city that murders the prophets. The city that stones those sent to help her. How often I have wanted to gather your children together even as a hen protects her brood under her wings, but you wouldn't let me. And now—now your house is left desolate. And you will never again see me until you say, 'Welcome to him who comes in the name of the Lord.' "

CHAPTER FOURTEEN

Advice

ONE SABBATH as Jesus was in the home of a member of the Jewish Council, the Pharisees were watching him like hawks to see if he would heal a man who was present who was suffering from dropsy.

Jesus said to the Pharisees and legal experts standing around, "Well, is it within the Law to heal a man on the Sabbath day, or not?"

And when they refused to answer, Jesus took the sick man by the hand and healed him and sent him away.

Then he turned to them: "Which of you doesn't work on the Sabbath?" he asked. "If your cow falls into a pit, don't you proceed at once to get it out?"

Again they had no answer.

When he noticed that all who came to the dinner were trying to sit near the head of the table, he gave them this advice: "If you are invited to a wedding feast, don't always head for the best seat. For if someone more respected than you shows up, the host will bring him over to where you are sitting and say, 'Let this man sit here instead.' And you, embarrassed, will have to take whatever seat is left at the foot of the table!

"Do this instead—start at the foot; and when your host sees you he will come and say, 'Friend, we have a better place than this for you!' Thus you will be honored in front of all the other guests. For everyone who tries to honor himself shall be humbled; and he who humbles himself shall be honored." Then he turned to his host. "When you put on a dinner," he said, "don't invite friends, brothers, relatives, and rich neighbors! For they will return the invitation. Instead, invite the poor, the crippled, the lame, and the blind. Then at the resurrection of the godly, God will reward you for inviting those who can't repay you."

Hearing this, a man sitting at the table with Jesus exclaimed, "What a privilege it would be to get into the Kingdom of God!"

Jesus replied with this illustration: "A man prepared a great feast and sent out many invitations. When all was ready, he sent his servant around to notify the guests that it was time for them to arrive. But they all began making excuses. One said he had just bought a field and wanted to inspect it, and asked to be excused. Another said he had just bought five pair of oxen and wanted to try them out. Another had just been married and for that reason couldn't come.

"The servant returned and reported to his master what they had said. His master was angry and told him to go quickly into the streets and alleys of the city and to invite the beggars, crippled, lame, and blind. But even then, there was still room.

" 'Well, then,' " said his master, 'go out into the country lanes and out behind the hedges and urge anyone you find to come, so that the house will be full. For none of those I invited first will get even the smallest taste of what I had prepared for them.' "

Great crowds were following him. He turned around and addressed them as follows: "Anyone who wants to be my follower must love me far more than he does his own father, mother, wife, children, brothers, or sisters—yes, more than his own life—otherwise he cannot be my disciple. And no one can be my disciple who does not carry his own cross and follow me.

"But don't begin until you count the cost. For who would begin construction of a building without first getting estimates and then checking to see if he has enough money to pay the bills? Otherwise he might complete only the foundation before running out of funds. And then how everyone would laugh!

" 'See that fellow there?' they would mock. 'He started that building and ran out of money before it was finished!'

"Or what king would ever dream of going to war without first sitting down with his counselors and discussing whether his army of 10,000 is strong enough to defeat the 20,000 men who are marching against him?

"If the decision is negative, then while the enemy troops are still far away, he will send a truce team to discuss terms of peace. So no one can become my disciple unless he first sits down and counts his blessings—and then renounces them all for me.

"What good is salt that has lost its saltiness? Flavorless salt is fit for nothing—not even for fertilizer. It is worthless and must be thrown out. Listen well, if you would understand my meaning."

CHAPTER FIFTEEN

Two Sons

DISHONEST TAX COLLECTORS and other notorious sinners often came to listen to Jesus' sermons; but this caused complaints from the Jewish religious leaders and the experts on Jewish law because he was associating with such despicable people—even eating with them! So Jesus used this illustration: "If you had a hundred sheep and one of them strayed away and was lost in the wilderness, wouldn't you leave the ninety-nine others to go and search for the lost one until you found it? And then you would joyfully carry it home on your shoulders. When you arrived you would call together your friends and neighbors to rejoice with you because your lost sheep was found.

"Well, in the same way heaven will be happier over one lost sinner who returns to God than over ninety-nine others who haven't strayed away!

"Or take another illustration: A woman has ten valuable silver coins and loses one. Won't she light a lamp and look in every corner of the house and sweep every nook and cranny until she finds it? And then won't she call in her friends and neighbors to rejoice with her? In the same way there is joy in the presence of the angels of God when one sinner repents."

To illustrate the point further, he told them this story: "A man had two sons. When the younger told his father, 'I want my share of your estate now, instead of waiting until you die!' his father agreed to divide his wealth between his sons.

"A few days later this younger son packed all his belongings and took a trip to a distant land, and there wasted all his money on parties and prostitutes. About the time his money was gone a great famine swept over the land, and he began to starve. He persuaded a local farmer to hire him to feed his pigs. The boy became so hungry that even the pods he was feeding the swine looked good to him. And no one gave him anything.

"When he finally came to his senses, he said to himself, 'At home even the hired men have food enough and to spare, and here I am, dying of hunger! I will go home to my father and say, "Father, I have sinned against both heaven and you, and am no longer worthy of being called your son. Please take me on as a hired man." '

"So he returned home to his father. And while he was still a long distance away, his father saw him coming, and was filled with loving pity and ran and embraced him and kissed him.

"His son said to him, 'Father, I have sinned against heaven and you, and am not worthy of being called your son—'

"But his father told the servants, 'Quick! Bring the finest robe in the house and put it on him. And a jeweled ring for his finger; and shoes! And kill the calf we have in the fattening pen. We must celebrate with a feast, for this son of mine was dead and has returned to life. He was lost and is found.' So the party began.

"Meanwhile, the older son was in the fields working; when he returned home, he heard dance music coming from the house, and he asked one of the servants what was going on.

" 'Your brother is back,' he was told, 'and your father has killed the calf we were fattening and has prepared a great feast to celebrate his coming home again unharmed.'

"The older brother was angry and wouldn't go in. His father came out and begged him, but he replied, 'All these years I've worked hard for you and never once refused to do a single thing you told me to; and in all that time you never gave me even one young goat for a feast with my friends. Yet when this son of yours comes back after spending your money on prostitutes, you celebrate by killing the finest calf we have on the place.'

" 'Look, dear son,' his father said to him, 'you and I are very close, and everything I have is yours. But it is right to celebrate. For he is your brother; and he was dead and has come back to life! He was lost and is found!' "

CHAPTER SIXTEEN

Evil Hearts

JESUS NOW TOLD this story to his disciples: "A rich man hired an accountant to handle his affairs, but soon a rumor went around that the accountant was thoroughly dishonest.

"So his employer called him in and said, 'What's this I hear about your stealing from me? Get your report in order, for you are to be dismissed.'

"The accountant thought to himself, 'Now what? I'm through here, and I haven't the strength to go out and dig ditches, and I'm too proud to beg. I know just the thing! And then I'll have plenty of friends to take care of me when I leave!'

"So he invited each one who owed money to his employer to come and discuss the situation. He asked the first one, 'How much do you owe him?' 'My debt is 850 gallons of olive oil,' the man replied. 'Yes, here is the contract you signed,' the accountant told him. 'Tear it up and write another one for half that much!'

" 'And how much do you owe him?' he asked the next man. 'A thousand bushels of wheat,' was the reply. 'Here,' the accountant said, 'take your note and replace it with one for only

800 bushels!'

"The rich man had to admire the rascal for being so shrewd. And it is true that the citizens of this world are more clever in dishonesty than the godly are. But shall I tell *you* to act that way, to buy friendship through cheating? Will this ensure your entry into an everlasting home in heaven? *No!* For unless you are honest in small matters, you won't be in large ones. If you cheat even a little, you won't be honest with greater responsibilities. And if you are untrustworthy about worldy wealth, who will trust you with the true riches of heaven? And if you are not faithful with other people's money, why should you be entrusted with money of your own?

"For neither you nor anyone else can serve two masters. You will hate one and show loyalty to the other, or else the other way around—you will be enthusiastic about one and despise the other. You cannot serve both God and money."

The Pharisees, who dearly loved their money, naturally scoffed at all this.

Then he said to them, "You wear a noble, pious expression in public, but God knows your evil hearts. Your pretense brings you honor from the people, but it is an abomination in the sight of God. Until John the Baptist began to preach, the laws of Moses and the messages of the prophets were your guides. But John introduced the Good News that the Kingdom of God would come soon. And now eager multitudes are pressing in. But that doesn't mean that the Law has lost its force in even the smallest point. It is as strong and unshakable as heaven and earth.

"So anyone who divorces his wife and marries someone else commits adultery, and anyone who marries a divorced woman commits adultery."

"There was a certain rich man," Jesus said, "who was splendidly clothed and lived each day in mirth and luxury. One day Lazarus, a diseased beggar, was laid at his door. As he lay there longing for scraps from the rich man's table, the dogs would come and lick his open sores. Finally the beggar died and was carried by the angels to be with Abraham in the place of the righteous dead. The rich man also died and was buried, and his soul went into hell. There, in torment, he saw Lazarus in the far distance with Abraham.

" 'Father Abraham,' he shouted, 'have some pity! Send Lazarus over here if only to dip the tip of his finger in water and cool my tongue, for I am in anguish in these flames.'

"But Abraham said to him, 'Son, remember that during your lifetime you had everything you wanted, and Lazarus had nothing. So now he is here being comforted and you are in anguish. And besides, there is a great chasm separating us, and anyone wanting to come to you from here is stopped at its edge; and no one over there can cross to us.'

"Then the rich man said, 'O Father Abraham, then please send him to my father's home—for I have five brothers—to warn them about this place of torment lest they come here when they die.'

"But Abraham said, 'The Scriptures have warned them again and again. Your brothers can read them any time they want to.'

"The rich man replied, 'No, Father Abraham, they won't bother to read them. But if someone is sent to them from the dead, then they will turn from their sins.'

"But Abraham said, 'If they won't listen to Moses and the prophets, they won't listen even though someone rises from the dead.' "

CHAPTER SEVENTEEN

Business as Usual

T HERE WILL ALWAYS be temptations to sin," Jesus said one day to his disciples, "but woe to the man who does the tempting. If he were thrown into the sea with a huge rock tied to his neck, he would be far better off than facing the punishment in store for those who harm little children's souls. I am warning you!

"Rebuke your brother if he sins, and forgive him if he is sorry. Even if he wrongs you seven times a day and each time turns again and asks forgiveness, forgive him."

One day the apostles said to the Lord, "We need more faith; tell us how to get it."

"If your faith were only the size of a mustard seed," Jesus answered, "it would be large enough to uproot that mulberry tree over there and send it hurtling into the sea! Your command would bring immediate results! When a servant comes in from plowing or taking care of sheep, he doesn't just sit down and eat, but first prepares his master's meal and serves him his supper before he eats his own. And he is not even thanked, for he is merely doing what he is supposed to do. Just so, if you merely obey me, you should not consider yourselves worthy of praise. For you have simply done your duty!"

As they continued onward toward Jerusalem, they reached the border between Galilee and Samaria, and as they entered a village there, ten lepers stood at a distance, crying out, "Jesus, sir, have mercy on us!"

He looked at them and said, "Go to the Jewish priest and show him that you are healed!" And as they were going, their leprosy disappeared.

One of them came back to Jesus, shouting, "Glory to God, I'm healed!" He fell flat on the ground in front of Jesus, face downward in the dust, thanking him for what he had done. This man was a despised Samaritan.

Jesus asked, "Didn't I heal ten men? Where are the nine? Does only this foreigner return to give glory to God?"

And Jesus said to the man, "Stand up and go; your faith has made you well."

One day the Pharisees asked Jesus, "When will the Kingdom of God begin?" Jesus replied, "The Kingdom of God isn't ushered in with visible signs. You won't be able to say, 'It has begun here in this place or there in that part of the country.' For the Kingdom of God is within you."

Later he talked again about this with his disciples. "The time is coming when you will long for me to be with you even for a single day, but I won't be here," he said. "Reports will reach you that I have returned and that I am in this place or that; don't believe it or go out to look for me. For when I return, you will know it beyond all doubt. It will be as evident as the lightning that flashes across the skies. But first I must suffer terribly and be rejected by this whole nation.

"When I return the world will be as indifferent to the things of God as the people were in Noah's day. They ate and drank and married—everything just as usual right up to the day when Noah went into the ark and the flood came and destroyed them all.

"And the world will be as it was in the days of Lot: people went about their daily business—eating and drinking, buying and selling, farming and building—until the morning Lot left Sodom. Then fire and brimstone rained down from heaven and destroyed them all. Yes, it will be 'business as usual' right up to the hour of my return.

"Those away from home that day must not return to pack; those in the fields must not return to town—remember what happened to Lot's wife! Whoever clings to his life shall lose it, and whoever loses his life shall save it. That night two men will be asleep in the same room, and one will be taken away, the other left. Two women will be working together at household tasks; one will be taken, the other left; and so it will be with men working side by side in the fields."

"Lord, where will they be taken?" the disciples asked.

Jesus replied, "Where the body is, the vultures gather!"

CHAPTER EIGHTEEN

Talking in Riddles

ONE DAY JESUS TOLD his disciples a story to illustrate their need for constant prayer and to show them that they must keep praying until the answer comes.

"There was a city judge," he said, "a very godless man who had great contempt for everyone. A widow of that city came to him frequently to appeal for justice against a man who had harmed her. The judge ignored her for a while, but eventually she got on his nerves.

" 'I fear neither God nor man,' he said to himself, 'but this woman bothers me. I'm going to see that she gets justice, for she is wearing me out with her constant coming!' "

Then the Lord said, "If even an evil judge can be worn down like that, don't you think that God will surely give justice to his people who plead with him day and night? Yes! He will answer them quickly! But the question is: When I, the Messiah, return, how many will I find who have faith and are praying?"

Then he told this story to some who boasted of their virtue and scorned everyone else:

"Two men went to the Temple to pray. One was a proud, self-righteous Pharisee, and the other a cheating tax collector. The proud Pharisee 'prayed' this prayer: 'Thank God, I am not a sinner like everyone else, especially like that tax collector over there! For I never cheat, I don't commit adultery, I go without food twice a week, and I give to God a tenth of everything I earn.'

"But the corrupt tax collector stood at a distance and dared not even lift his eyes to heaven as he prayed, but beat upon his chest in sorrow, exclaiming, 'God, be merciful to me, a sinner.' I tell you, this sinner, not the Pharisee, returned home forgiven! For the proud shall be humbled, but the humble shall be honored."

One day some mothers brought their babies to him to touch and bless. But the disciples told them to go away.

Then Jesus called the children over to him and said to the disciples, "Let the little children come to me! Never send them away! For the Kingdom of God belongs to men who have hearts as trusting as these little children's. And anyone who doesn't have their kind of faith will never get within the Kingdom's gates."

Once a Jewish religious leader asked him this question: "Good sir, what shall I do to get to heaven?"

"Do you realize what you are saying when you call me 'good'?" Jesus asked him. "Only God is truly good, and no one else.

"But as to your question, you know what the ten commandments say—don't commit adultery, don't murder, don't steal, don't lie, honor your parents, and so on." The man replied, "I've obeyed every one of these laws since I was a small child."

"There is still one thing you lack," Jesus said. "Sell all you have and give the money to the poor—it will become treasure for you in heaven—and come, follow me."

But when the man heard this he went sadly away, for he was very rich.

Jesus watched him go and then said to his disciples, "How

hard it is for the rich to enter the Kingdom of God! It is easier for a camel to go through the eye of a needle than for a rich man to enter the Kingdom of God."

Those who heard him say this exclaimed, "If it is that hard, how can *anyone* be saved?"

He replied, "God can do what men can't!"

And Peter said, "We have left our homes and followed you."

"Yes," Jesus replied, "and everyone who has done as you have, leaving home, wife, brothers, parents, or children for the sake of the Kingdom of God, will be repaid many times over now, as well as receiving eternal life in the world to come."

Gathering the Twelve around him he told them, "As you know, we are going to Jerusalem. And when we get there, all the predictions of the ancient prophets concerning me will come true. I will be handed over to the Gentiles to be mocked and treated shamefully and spat upon, and lashed and killed. And the third day I will rise again."

But they didn't understand a thing he said. He seemed to be talking in riddles.

As they approached Jericho, a blind man was sitting beside the road, begging from travelers. When he heard the noise of a crowd going past, he asked what was happening. He was told that Jesus from Nazareth was going by, so he began shouting, "Jesus, Son of David, have mercy on me!"

The crowds ahead of Jesus tried to hush the man, but he only yelled the louder, "Son of David, have mercy on me!"

When Jesus arrived at the spot, he stopped. "Bring the blind man over here," he said. Then Jesus asked the man, "What do you want?"

"Lord," he pleaded, "I want to see!"

And Jesus said, "All right, begin seeing! Your faith has healed you."

And instantly the man could see, and followed Jesus, praising God. And all who saw it happen praised God too.

CHAPTER NINETEEN

Procession

As JESUS WAS PASSING through Jericho, a man named Zacchaeus, one of the most influential Jews in the Roman tax-collecting business (and, of course, a very rich man), tried to get a look at Jesus, but he was too short to see over the crowds. So he ran ahead and climbed into a sycamore tree beside the road, to watch from there.

When Jesus came by he looked up at Zacchaeus and called him by name. "Zacchaeus!" he said. "Quick! Come down! For I am going to be a guest in your home today!"

Zacchaeus hurriedly climbed down and took Jesus to his house in great excitement and joy.

But the crowds were displeased. "He has gone to be the guest of a notorious sinner," they grumbled.

Meanwhile, Zacchaeus stood before the Lord and said, "Sir, from now on I will give half my wealth to the poor, and if I find I have overcharged anyone on his taxes, I will penalize myself by giving him back four times as much!"

Jesus told him, "This shows that salvation has come to this home today. This man was one of the lost sons of Abraham, and

I, the Messiah, have come to search for and to save such souls as his."

And because Jesus was nearing Jerusalem, he told a story to correct the impression that the Kingdom of God would begin right away.

"A nobleman living in a certain province was called away to the distant capital of the empire to be crowned king of his province. Before he left he called together ten assistants and gave them each $2,000 to invest while he was gone. But some of his people hated him and sent him their declaration of independence, stating that they had rebelled and would not acknowledge him as their king.

"Upon his return he called in the men to whom he had given the money, to find out what they had done with it, and what their profits were.

"The first man reported a tremendous gain—ten times as much as the original amount!

" 'Fine!' the king exclaimed. 'You are a good man. You have been faithful with the little I entrusted to you, and as your reward, you shall be governor of ten cities.'

"The next man also reported a splendid gain—five times the original amount.

" 'All right!' his master said. 'You can be governor over five cities.'

"But the third man brought back only the money he had started with. 'I've kept it safe,' he said, 'because I was afraid you would demand my profits, for you are a hard man to deal with, taking what isn't yours and even confiscating the crops that others plant.' 'You vile and wicked slave,' the king roared. 'Hard, am I? That's exactly how I'll be toward you! If you knew so much about me and how tough I am, then why didn't you deposit the money in the bank so that I could at least get some interest on it?'

"Then turning to the others standing by he ordered, 'Take the money away from him and give it to the man who earned the most.'

" 'But, sir,' they said, 'he has enough already!'

" 'Yes,' the king replied, 'but it is always true that those who have, get more, and those who have little, soon lose even that. And now about these enemies of mine who revolted—bring them in and execute them before me.' "

After telling this story, Jesus went on toward Jerusalem, walking along ahead of his disciples. As they came to the towns of Bethphage and Bethany, on the Mount of Olives, he sent two disciples ahead, with instructions to go to the next village, and as they entered they were to look for a donkey tied beside the road. It would be a colt, not yet broken for riding.

"Untie him," Jesus said, "and bring him here. And if anyone asks you what you are doing, just say, 'The Lord needs him.' "

They found the colt as Jesus said, and sure enough, as they were untying it, the owners demanded an explanation.

"What are you doing?" they asked. "Why are you untying our colt?"

And the disciples replied, "The Lord needs him!" So they brought the colt to Jesus and threw some of their clothing across its back for Jesus to sit on.

Then the crowds spread out their robes along the road ahead of him, and as they reached the place where the road started down from the Mount of Olives, the whole procession began to shout and sing as they walked along, praising God for all the wonderful miracles Jesus had done.

"God has given us a King!" they exulted. "Long live the King! Let all heaven rejoice! Glory to God in the highest heavens!"

But some of the Pharisees among the crowd said, "Sir, rebuke your followers for saying things like that!"

He replied, "If they keep quiet, the stones along the road will burst into cheers!"

But as they came closer to Jerusalem and he saw the city ahead, he began to cry. "Eternal peace was within your reach and you turned it down," he wept, "and now it is too late. Your enemies will pile up earth against your walls and encircle you and close in on you, and crush you to the ground, and your children within you; your enemies will not leave one stone upon another—for you have rejected the opportunity God offered you."

Then he entered the Temple and began to drive out the merchants from their stalls, saying to them, "The Scriptures declare, 'My Temple is a place of prayer; but you have turned it into a den of thieves.' "

After that he taught daily in the Temple, but the chief priests and other religious leaders and the business community were trying to find some way to get rid of him. But they could think of nothing, for he was a hero to the people—they hung on every word he said.

CHAPTER TWENTY

Questions

ON ONE OF THOSE DAYS when he was teaching and preaching the Good News in the Temple, he was confronted by the chief priests and other religious leaders and councilmen. They demanded to know by what authority he had driven out the merchants from the Temple.

"I'll ask you a question before I answer," he replied. "Was John sent by God, or was he merely acting under his own authority?"

They talked it over among themselves. "If we say his message was from heaven, then we are trapped because he will ask, 'Then why didn't you believe him?' But if we say John was not sent from God, the people will mob us, for they are convinced that he was a prophet." Finally they replied. "We don't know!"

And Jesus responded, "Then I won't answer your question either."

Now he turned to the people again and told them this story: "A man planted a vineyard and rented it out to some farmers, and went away to a distant land to live for several years. When harvest time came, he sent one of his men to the farm to collect his share of the crops. But the tenants beat him up and sent him back empty-handed. Then he sent another, but the same thing happened; he was beaten up and insulted and sent away without collecting. A third man was sent and the same thing happened. He, too, was wounded and chased away.

" 'What shall I do?' the owner asked himself. 'I know! I'll send my cherished son. Surely they will show respect for him.'

"But when the tenants saw his son, they said, 'This is our chance! This fellow will inherit all the land when his father dies. Come on. Let's kill him, and then it will be ours.' So they dragged him out of the vineyard and killed him.

"What do you think the owner will do? I'll tell you—he will come and kill them and rent the vineyard to others."

"But they would never do a thing like that," his listeners protested.

Jesus looked at them and said, "Then what does the Scripture mean where it says, 'The Stone rejected by the builders was made the cornerstone'?" And he added, "Whoever stumbles over that Stone shall be broken; and those on whom it falls will be crushed to dust."

When the chief priests and religious leaders heard about this story he had told, they wanted him arrested immediately, for they realized that he was talking about them. They were the wicked tenants in his illustration. But they were afraid that if they themselves arrested him there would be a riot. So they tried to get him to say something that could be reported to the Roman governor as reason for arrest by him.

Watching their opportunity, they sent secret agents pretending to be honest men. They said to Jesus, "Sir, we know what an honest teacher you are. You always tell the truth and don't budge an inch in the face of what others think, but teach the ways of God. Now tell us—is it right to pay taxes to the Roman government or not?"

He saw through their trickery and said, "Show me a coin. Whose portrait is this on it? And whose name?"

They replied, "Caesar's—the Roman emperor's."

He said, "Then give the emperor all that is his—and give to God all that is his!"

Thus their attempt to outwit him before the people failed; and marveling at his answer, they were silent.

Then some Sadducees—men who believed that death is the end of existence, that there is no resurrection—came to Jesus with this:

"The laws of Moses state that if a man dies without children, the man's brother shall marry the widow and their children will legally belong to the dead man, to carry on his name. We know of a family of seven brothers. The oldest married and then died without any children. His brother married the widow and he, too, died. Still no children. And so it went, one after the other, until each of the seven had married her and died, leaving no children. Finally the woman died also. Now here is our question: Whose wife will she be in the resurrection? For all of them were married to her!"

Jesus replied, "Marriage is for people here on earth, but when those who are counted worthy of being raised from the dead get to heaven, they do not marry. And they never die again; in these respects they are like angels, and are sons of God, for they are raised up in new life from the dead.

"But as to your real question—whether or not there is a resurrection—why, even the writings of Moses himself prove this. For when he describes how God appeared to him in the burning bush, he speaks of God as 'the God of Abraham, the God of Isaac, and the God of Jacob.' To say that the Lord *is* some person's God means that person is *alive*, not dead! So from God's point of view, all are living."

"Well said, sir!" remarked some of the experts in the Jewish law who were standing there. And that ended their questions, for they dared ask no more!

Then he presented *them* with a question. "Why is it," he asked, "that Christ, the Messiah, is said to be a descendant of

King David? For David himself wrote in the book of Psalms: 'God said to my Lord, the Messiah, "Sit at my right hand until I place your enemies beneath your feet." ' How can the Messiah be both David's son and David's God at the same time?"

Then, with the crowds listening, he turned to his disciples and said, "Beware of these experts in religion, for they love to parade in dignified robes and to be bowed to by the people as they walk along the street. And how they love the seats of honor in the synagogues and at religious festivals! But even while they are praying long prayers with great outward piety, they are planning schemes to cheat widows out of their property. Therefore God's heaviest sentence awaits these men."

CHAPTER TWENTY-ONE

In God's Good Time

As HE STOOD in the Temple, Jesus observed the rich tossing their gifts into the collection box. Then a poor widow came by and dropped in two small copper coins.

"Really," he remarked, "this poor widow has given more than all the rest of them combined. For they have given a little of what they didn't need, but she, poor as she is, has given everything she has."

Some of his disciples began talking about the beautiful stonework of the Temple and the memorial decorations on the walls.

But Jesus said, "The time is coming when all these things you are admiring will be knocked down, and not one stone will be left on top of another; all will become one vast heap of rubble."

"Master!" they exclaimed. "When? And will there be any warning ahead of time?"

He replied, "Don't let anyone mislead you. For many will come announcing themselves as the Messiah, and saying, 'The time has come.' But don't believe them! And when you hear of

wars and insurrections beginning, don't panic. True, wars must come, but the end won't follow immediately—for nation shall rise against nation and kingdom against kingdom, and there will be great earthquakes, and famines in many lands, and epidemics, and terrifying things happening in the heavens.

"But before all this occurs, there will be a time of special persecution, and you will be dragged into synagogues and prisons and before kings and governors for my name's sake. But as a result, the Messiah will be widely known and honored. Therefore, don't be concerned about how to answer the charges against you, for I will give you the right words and such logic that none of your opponents will be able to reply! Even those closest to you—your parents, brothers, relatives, and friends will betray you and have you arrested; and some of you will be killed. And everyone will hate you because you are mine and are called by my name. But not a hair of your head will perish! For if you stand firm, you will win your souls.

"But when you see Jerusalem surrounded by armies, then you will know that the time of its destruction has arrived. Then let the people of Judea flee to the hills. Let those in Jerusalem try to escape, and those outside the city must not attempt to return. For those will be days of God's judgment, and the words of the ancient Scriptures written by the prophets will be abundantly fulfilled. Woe to expectant mothers in those days, and those with tiny babies. For there will be great distress upon this nation and wrath upon this people. They will be brutally killed by enemy weapons, or sent away as exiles and captives to all the nations of the world; and Jerusalem shall be conquered and trampled down by the Gentiles until the period of Gentile triumph ends in God's good time.

"Then there will be strange events in the skies—warnings, evil omens and portents in the sun, moon and stars; and down here on earth the nations will be in turmoil, perplexed by the roaring seas and strange tides. The courage of many people will falter because of the fearful fate they see coming upon the earth, for the stability of the very heavens will be broken up. Then the peoples of the earth shall see me, the Messiah, coming in a cloud with power and great glory. So when all these things begin to happen, stand straight and look up! For your salvation is near."

Then he gave them this illustration: "Notice the fig tree, or any other tree. When the leaves come out, you know without being told that summer is near. In the same way, when you see the events taking place that I've described you can be just as sure that the Kingdom of God is near.

"I solemnly declare to you that when these things happen, the end of this age has come. And though all heaven and earth shall pass away, yet my words remain forever true.

"Watch out! Don't let my sudden coming catch you unawares; don't let me find you living in careless ease, carousing and drinking, and occupied with the problems of this life, like all the rest of the world. Keep a constant watch. And pray that if possible you may arrive in my presence without having to experience these horrors."

Every day Jesus went to the Temple to teach, and the crowds began gathering early in the morning to hear him. And each evening he returned to spend the night on the Mount of Olives.

CHAPTER TWENTY-TWO

When the Rooster Crows

AND NOW the Passover celebration was drawing near—the Jewish festival when only bread made without yeast was used. The chief priests and other religious leaders were actively plotting Jesus' murder, trying to find a way to kill him without starting a riot—a possibility they greatly feared.

Then Satan entered into Judas Iscariot, who was one of the twelve disciples, and he went over to the chief priests and captains of the Temple guards to discuss the best way to betray Jesus to them. They were, of course, delighted to know that he was ready to help them and promised him a reward. So he began to look for an opportunity for them to arrest Jesus quietly when the crowds weren't around.

Now the day of the Passover celebration arrived, when the Passover lamb was killed and eaten with the unleavened bread. Jesus sent Peter and John ahead to find a place to prepare their Passover meal.

"Where do you want us to go?" they asked.

And he replied, "As soon as you enter Jerusalem, you will see a man walking along carrying a pitcher of water. Follow him into the house he enters, and say to the man who lives there, 'Our Teacher says for you to show us the guest room where he can eat the Passover meal with his disciples.' He will take you upstairs to a large room all ready for us. That is the place. Go ahead and prepare the meal there."

They went off to the city and found everything just as Jesus had said, and prepared the Passover supper.

Then Jesus and the others arrived, and at the proper time all sat down together at the table; and he said, "I have looked forward to this hour with deep longing, anxious to eat this Passover meal with you before my suffering begins. For I tell you now that I won't eat it again until what it represents has occurred in the Kingdom of God."

Then he took a glass of wine, and when he had given thanks for it, he said, "Take this and share it among yourselves. For I will not drink wine again until the Kingdom of God has come." ·

Then he took a loaf of bread; and when he had thanked God for it, he broke it apart and gave it to them, saying, "This is my body, given for you. Eat it in remembrance of me."

After supper he gave them another glass of wine, saying, "This wine is the token of God's new agreement to save you—an agreement sealed with the blood I shall pour out to purchase back your souls. But here at this table, sitting among us as a friend, is the man who will betray me. I must die. It is part of God's plan. But, oh, the horror awaiting that man who betrays me."

Then the disciples wondered among themselves which of them would ever do such a thing.

And they began to argue among themselves as to who would have the highest rank in the coming Kingdom.

Jesus told them, "In this world the kings and great men order their slaves around, and the slaves have no choice but to like it! But among you, the one who serves you best will be your leader. Out in the world the master sits at the table and is served by his servants. But not here! For I am your servant. Nevertheless, because you have stood true to me in these terrible days, and because my Father has granted me a Kingdom, I, here and now, grant you the right to eat and drink at my table in that Kingdom; and you will sit on thrones judging the twelve tribes of Israel.

"Simon, Simon, Satan has asked to have you, to sift you like wheat, but I have pleaded in prayer for you that your faith should not completely fail. So when you have repented and turned to me again, strengthen and build up the faith of your brothers."

Simon said, "Lord, I am ready to go to jail with you, and even to die with you."

But Jesus said, "Peter, let me tell you something. Between now and tomorrow morning when the rooster crows, you will deny me three times, declaring that you don't even know me."

Then Jesus asked them, "When I sent you out to preach the Good News and you were without money, duffle bag, or extra clothing, how did you get along?"

"Fine," they replied.

"But now," he said, "take a duffle bag if you have one, and your money. And if you don't have a sword, better sell your clothes and buy one! For the time has come for this prophecy about me to come true: 'He will be condemned as a criminal!' Yes, everything written about me by the prophets will come true."

"Master," they replied, "we have two swords among us."

"Enough!" he said.

Then, accompanied by the disciples, he left the upstairs room and went as usual to the Mount of Olives. There he told them, "Pray God that you will not be overcome by temptation."

He walked away, perhaps a stone's throw, and knelt down and prayed this prayer: "Father, if you are willing, please take away this cup of horror from me. But I want your will, not mine." Then an angel from heaven appeared and strengthened him, for he was in such agony of spirit that he broke into a sweat of blood, with great drops falling to the ground as he prayed more and more earnestly. At last he stood up again and returned to the disciples—only to find them asleep, exhausted from grief.

"Asleep!" he said. "Get up! Pray God that you will not fall when you are tempted."

But even as he said this, a mob approached, led by Judas, one of his twelve disciples. Judas walked over to Jesus and kissed him on the cheek in friendly greeting.

But Jesus said, "Judas, how can you do this—betray the Messiah with a kiss?"

When the other disciples saw what was about to happen, they exclaimed, "Master, shall we fight? We brought along the swords!" And one of them slashed at the High Priest's servant, and cut off his right ear.

But Jesus said, "Don't resist any more." And he touched the place where the man's ear had been and restored it. Then Jesus addressed the chief priests and captains of the Temple guards and the religious leaders who headed the mob. "Am I a robber," he asked, "that you have come armed with swords and clubs to get me? Why didn't you arrest me in the Temple? I was there every day. But this is your moment—the time when Satan's power reigns supreme."

So they seized him and led him to the High Priest's residence, and Peter followed at a distance. The soldiers lit a fire in the courtyard and sat around it for warmth, and Peter joined them there.

A servant girl noticed him in the firelight and began staring at him. Finally she spoke: "This man was with Jesus!"

Peter denied it. "Woman," he said, "I don't even know the man!"

After a while someone else looked at him and said, "You must be one of them!"

"No sir, I am not!" Peter replied.

About an hour later someone else flatly stated, 'I know this fellow is one of Jesus' disciples, for both are from Galilee."

But Peter said, "Man, I don't know what you are talking about." And as he said the words, a rooster crowed.

At that moment Jesus turned and looked at Peter. Then Peter remembered what he had said—"Before the rooster crows tomorrow morning, you will deny me three times." And Peter walked out of the courtyard, crying bitterly.

Now the guards in charge of Jesus began mocking him. They blindfolded him and hit him with their fists and asked, "Who hit you that time, prophet?" And they threw all sorts of other insults at him.

Early the next morning at daybreak the Jewish Supreme Court assembled, including the chief priests and all the top religious authorities of the nation. Jesus was led before this Council, and instructed to state whether or not he claimed to be the Messiah.

But he replied, "If I tell you, you won't believe me or let me present my case. But the time is soon coming when I, the Messiah, shall be enthroned beside Almighty God."

They all shouted, "Then you claim you are the Son of God?"

And he replied, "Yes, I am."

"What need do we have for other witnesses?" they shouted. "For we ourselves have heard him say it."

CHAPTER TWENTY-THREE

A Place Called 'the Skull'

THEN THE ENTIRE Council took Jesus over to Pilate, the governor. They began at once accusing him: "This fellow has been leading our people to ruin by telling them not to pay their taxes to the Roman government and by claiming he is our Messiah—a King."

So Pilate asked him, "Are you their Messiah—their King?"

"Yes," Jesus replied, "it is as you say."

Then Pilate turned to the chief priests and to the mob and said, "So? That isn't a crime!"

Then they became desperate. "But he is causing riots against the government everywhere he goes, all over Judea, from Galilee to Jerusalem!"

"Is he then a Galilean?" Pilate asked.

When they told him yes, Pilate said to take him to King Herod, for Galilee was under Herod's jurisdiction; and Herod happened to be in Jerusalem at the time. Herod was delighted at the opportunity to see Jesus, for he had heard a lot about him and had been hoping to see him perform a miracle.

He asked Jesus question after question, but there was no reply. Meanwhile, the chief priests and the other religious leaders stood there shouting their accusations.

Now Herod and his soldiers began mocking and ridiculing Jesus; and putting a kingly robe on him, they sent him back to Pilate. That day Herod and Pilate—enemies before—became fast friends.

Then Pilate called together the chief priests and other Jewish leaders, along with the people, and announced his verdict:

"You brought this man to me, accusing him of leading a revolt against the Roman government. I have examined him thoroughly on this point and find him innocent. Herod came to the same conclusion and sent him back to us—nothing this man has done calls for the death penalty. I will therefore have him scourged with leaded thongs, and release him."

But now a mighty roar rose from the crowd as with one voice they shouted, "Kill him, and release Barabbas to us!" (Barabbas was in prison for starting an insurrection in Jerusalem against the government, and for murder.) Pilate argued with them, for he wanted to release Jesus. But they shouted, "Crucify him! Crucify him!"

Once more, for the third time, he demanded, "Why? What crime has he committed? I have found no reason to sentence him to death. I will therefore scourge him and let him go." But they shouted louder and louder for Jesus' death, and their voices prevailed.

So Pilate sentenced Jesus to die as they demanded. And he released Barabbas, the man in prison for insurrection and murder, at their request. But he delivered Jesus over to them to do with as they would.

As the crowd led Jesus away to his death, Simon of Cyrene, who was just coming into Jerusalem from the country, was forced to follow, carrying Jesus' cross. Great crowds trailed along behind, and many grief-stricken women.

But Jesus turned and said to them, "Daughters of Jerusalem, don't weep for me, but for yourselves and for your children. For the days are coming when the women who have no children will be counted fortunate indeed. Mankind will beg the mountains to fall on them and crush them, and the hills to bury them. For if such things as this are done to me, the Living Tree, what will they do to you?"

Two others, criminals, were led out to be executed with him at a place called "The Skull." There all three were crucified—Jesus on the center cross, and the two criminals on either side.

"Father, forgive these people," Jesus said, "for they don't know what they are doing."

And the soldiers gambled for his clothing, throwing dice for each piece. The crowd watched. And the Jewish leaders laughed and scoffed. "He was so good at helping others," they said, "let's see him save himself if he is really God's Chosen One, the Messiah."

The soldiers mocked him, too, by offering him a drink—of sour wine. And they called to him, "If you are the King of the Jews, save yourself!"

A signboard was nailed to the cross above him with these words: "This is the King of the Jews."

One of the criminals hanging beside him scoffed. "So you're the Messiah, are you? Prove it by saving yourself—and us, too, while you're at it!"

But the other criminal protested. "Don't you even fear God when you are dying? We deserve to die for our evil deeds, but this man hasn't done one thing wrong." Then he said, "Jesus, remember me when you come into your Kingdom."

And Jesus replied, "Today you will be with me in Paradise. This is a solemn promise."

By now it was noon, and darkness fell across the whole land for three hours, until three o'clock. The light from the sun was gone—and suddenly the thick veil hanging in the Temple split apart.

Then Jesus shouted, "Father, I commit my spirit to you," and with those words he died.

When the captain of the Roman military unit handling the executions saw what had happened, he was stricken with awe before God and said, "Surely this man was innocent."

And when the crowd that came to see the crucifixion saw that Jesus was dead, they went home in deep sorrow. Meanwhile, Jesus' friends, including the women who had followed him down from Galilee, stood in the distance watching.

Then a man named Joseph, a member of the Jewish Supreme Court, from the city of Arimathea in Judea, went to Pilate and asked for the body of Jesus. He was a godly man who had been expecting the Messiah's coming and had not agreed with the decision and actions of the other Jewish leaders. So he took down Jesus' body and wrapped it in a long linen cloth and laid it in a new, unused tomb hewn into the rock at the side of a hill. This was done late on Friday afternoon, the day of preparation for the Sabbath.

As the body was taken away, the women from Galilee followed and saw it carried into the tomb. Then they went home and prepared spices and ointments to embalm him; but by the time they were finished it was the Sabbath, so they rested all that day as required by the Jewish law.

CHAPTER TWENTY-FOUR

Time of Glory

BUT VERY EARLY on Sunday morning the women took the ointments to the tomb—and found that the huge stone covering the entrance had been rolled aside. So they went in—but the Lord Jesus' body was gone.

They stood there puzzled, trying to think what could have happened to it. Suddenly two men appeared before them, clothed in shining robes so bright their eyes were dazzled. The women were terrified and bowed low before them.

Then the men asked, "Why are you looking in a tomb for someone who is alive? He isn't here! He has come back to life again! Don't you remember what he told you back in Galilee—that the Messiah must be betrayed into the power of evil men and be crucified and that he would rise again the third day?"

Then they remembered, and rushed back to Jerusalem to tell his eleven disciples—and everyone else—what had happened. (The women who went to the tomb were Mary Magdalene and Joanna and Mary the mother of James, and several others.) But the story sounded like a fairy tale to the men—they didn't believe it.

However, Peter ran to the tomb to look. Stooping, he peered in and saw the empty linen wrappings; and then he went back home again, wondering what had happened.

That same day, Sunday, two of Jesus' followers were walking to the village of Emmaus, seven miles out of Jerusalem. As they walked along they were talking of Jesus' death, when suddenly Jesus himself came along and joined them and began walking beside them. But they didn't recognize him, for God kept them from it.

"You seem to be in a deep discussion about something," he said. "What are you so concerned about?" They stopped short, sadness written across their faces. And one of them, Cleopas, replied, "You must be the only person in Jerusalem who hasn't heard about the terrible things that happened there last week."

"What things?" Jesus asked.

"The things that happened to Jesus, the Man from Nazareth," they said. "He was a Prophet who did incredible miracles and was a mighty Teacher, highly regarded by both God and man. But the chief priests and our religious leaders arrested him and handed him over to the Roman government to be condemned to death, and they crucified him. We had thought he was the glorious Messiah and that he had come to rescue Israel.

"And now, besides all this—which happened three days ago—some women from our group of his followers were at his tomb early this morning and came back with an amazing report that his body was missing, and that they had seen some angels there who told them Jesus is alive! Some of our men ran out to see, and sure enough, Jesus' body was gone, just as the women had said."

Then Jesus said to them, "You are such foolish, foolish people! You find it so hard to believe all that the prophets wrote in the Scriptures! Wasn't it clearly predicted by the prophets that the Messiah would have to suffer all these things before entering his time of glory?"

Then Jesus quoted them passage after passage from the writings of the prophets, beginning with the book of Genesis and going right on through the Scriptures, explaining what the passages meant and what they said about himself.

By this time they were nearing Emmaus and the end of their journey. Jesus would have gone on, but they begged him to stay the night with them, as it was getting late. So he went home with them. As they sat down to eat, he asked God's blessing on the food and then took a small loaf of bread and broke it and was passing it over to them, when suddenly—it was as though their eyes were opened—they recognized him! And at that moment he disappeared.

They began telling each other how their hearts had felt strangely warm as he talked with them and explained the Scriptures during the walk down the road. Within the hour they were on their way back to Jerusalem, where the eleven disciples and the other followers of Jesus greeted them with these words, "The Lord has really risen! He appeared to Peter!"

Then the two from Emmaus told their story of how Jesus had appeared to them as they were walking along the road and how they had recognized him as he was breaking the bread. And just as they were telling about it, Jesus himself was suddenly standing there among them, and greeted them. But the whole group was terribly frightened, thinking they were seeing a ghost!

"Why are you frightened?" he asked. "Why do you doubt that it is really I? Look at my hands! Look at my feet! You can see that it is I, myself! Touch me and make sure that I am not a ghost! For ghosts don't have bodies, as you see that I do!" As he spoke, he held out his hands for them to see the marks of the nails, and showed them the wounds in his feet.

Still they stood there undecided, filled with joy and doubt.

Then he asked them, "Do you have anything here to eat?"

They gave him a piece of broiled fish, and he ate it as they watched.

Then he said, "When I was with you before, don't you remember my telling you that everything written about me by

Moses and the prophets and in the Psalms must all come true?"
Then he opened their minds to understand at last these many
Scriptures! And he said, "Yes, it was written long ago that the
Messiah must suffer and die and rise again from the dead on the
third day; and that this message of salvation should be taken
from Jerusalem to all the nations: *There is forgiveness of sins
for all who turn to me.* You have seen these prophecies come
true.

"And now I will send the Holy Spirit upon you, just as my
Father promised. Don't begin telling others yet—stay here in
the city until the Holy Spirit comes and fills you with power
from heaven."

Then Jesus led them out along the road to Bethany, and lift-
ing his hands to heaven, he blessed them, and then began rising
into the sky, and went on to heaven. And they worshiped him,
and returned to Jerusalem filled with mighty joy, and were con-
tinually in the Temple, praising God.

About the Author

LUKE WAS GREEK by birth. The Gospel here reprinted was written by him in the Greek language for Greek-speaking readers. He was well educated—perhaps a "physician" and an early convert to Christianity. He did not himself witness the events he writes about in the Gospel, but he was a companion to St. Paul on missionary journeys to Asia Minor, Greece, and Italy. He gathered information about the life and teachings of Jesus from various writings of eyewitnesses and from the companions of Jesus who were still living.

In about the year 63, he wrote his Gospel. It has been called "the most beautiful book ever written." Soon after, he wrote a second book about the events in the early Church between the time of Jesus' death (30?) and that of Paul's last imprisonment in Rome (63?). This second book is a continuation of the story told in Luke's Gospel and appears in the New Testament as the "Acts of the Apostles."

Luke dedicated both his Gospel and his Acts of the Apostles to a man named Theophilus (the name means "one who loves God"). Luke addressed him as "Most Excellent," which was at that time the way in which high Roman officials were addressed. Theophilus may have sponsored Luke's writings and arranged to have copies of them sent to Greek-speaking Christian communities. There is a tradition that Luke never married and that he lived till the age of 84. The feast day for St. Luke is October 18.

DATE DUE

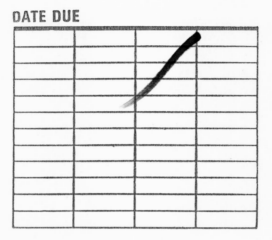

DEMCO